MW01611556

DAILY PRAYERS *for* SERVANT LEADERS

SPIRITUAL STRENGTH
FOR AUTHENTIC ACHIEVEMENT

Richard P. Johnson, Ph.D.

Gary H. Ferbet, D.Min.

ISBN 978-0-9903384-0-6

10 9 8 7 6 5 4 3 2 1

First Edition

Cover design by Megan Irwin

Edited by Maggie Singleton

Printed in the United States of America

Contents

Introduction

"Jesus called them together and said, 'You know that those who are regarded as rulers of the Gentiles lord it over them, and their high officials exercise authority over them. Not so with you. Instead, whoever wants to become great among you must be your servant, and whoever wants to be first must be servant of all. For even the Son of Man did not come to be served, but to serve, and to give his life as a ransom for many.'" ~ Mark 10:42-45

Prayer: Your Most Powerful Leadership Tool

Prayer makes you more receptive; it softens your soul, prepares your mind, and sensitizes your heart in ways that allow you a fuller flow of grace through God's conduits of love. ~ Dr. Johnson

Servant Leadership in any church or faith-based organization requires that you tap into your motivated spiritual strengths. Regardless of your position, if your decisions and actions move and lead others in any way, then you are a leader. And Servant Leadership, or Christ-based leadership; is the most effective form of leadership there is; and your most powerful motivating tool in your leadership position is prayer!

If the local church is the hope of the world, Servant Leadership is the performance engine that fulfills biblical mandates and brings tangible results to the local church and other faith-based organization, and hence to the kingdom in time. To achieve this we rely on God's grace through prayer.

As a Servant Leader, you are an agent of hope, health, and healing in a broken world, you are a "point-of-light" that guides, motivates,

5

and moves organizations of faith to take up their given mission and serve not only the common good, but the greater, divine good. Perhaps the number one prerequisite of true Servant Leadership is being "tuned-in" to their inner core, to their God-given spiritual uniqueness. To accomplish all this you need God's grace; you need to actively open up your portals of grace and receive this most animating energy from God. This is the province of prayer.

Your church, organization, hospital, or association is a dynamic living entity, and its lifeblood begins in the faith-filled hearts of its Servant Leaders. Servant Leadership is essentially a journey of expanding faith—a journey of self-discovery, improved self-understanding, and eventually a new dynamic way of being in this world. This too is the province of prayer.

Prayer and Servant Leadership

Prayer helps you express your special contributions more clearly and mobilize the strengths in others whom you serve. ~ Greenleaf, 1976.

Prayer affects so many facets of who you are as a Servant Leader. According to the Spiritual Strengths Healing Plan, or SSHP, your advancing relationship with the divine will yield interior changes in six different, yet intimately connected areas (functions) of your personality:

1. Prayer helps you believe deeper; it gives you a new internal framework for your organization, the people in it, and yourself in entirely new ways (Autry, 2001).

2. Prayer helps you see better by developing a clearer vision of what's most important, and gaining new insights into what is needed next.

3. Prayer helps you think more accurately by opening up your mind in new ways to consider new possibilities.

4. Prayer helps you <u>feel</u> with compassion so you can better walk in another's shoes (Daloz-Parks, 2005).

5. Prayer helps you make better <u>decisions</u> by facilitating choices that are more closely consistent with all the variables and factors that surround any issue. Prayer also helps you steer away from making simplistic choices that satisfy some but alienate others.

6. Finally, prayer helps you take <u>action</u> in ways that further the overall mission and vision of the organization and raise both the common good and the divine good.

Journeying to the core of who you are, through the power of the Holy Spirit, prayer can help you believe, perceive, think, feel, decide, and act in ways you never thought possible. This central belief of the SSHP will illuminate your Servant Leadership in new and powerful ways. See Appendix III to gain a better understanding of how the strengths mentioned in this prayer book operate within you and through you—using the amalgamation of gifts God has bestowed upon you.

"I have been indebted to Dr. Johnson for years as he has shared his research, conducted over a span of years as the Director of Behavioral Sciences at a large metropolitan medical center. His many books have instructed me and thousands of others about the movement and effect of God's power in our lives. The outcome of his teaching has not remained theoretical in my life, but has indeed transformed (healed) me." ~ Gary Ferbet

---

Organization of the Book

The prayers in this volume are presented in sets of three. The first prayer in each set, the Morning Prayer, focuses on a particular spiritual strength (virtue). The second prayer, or Afternoon Prayer, focuses on the "shadow" of that spiritual strength; while the third prayer, the Evening Prayer, focuses on the "compulsion" of that spiritual strength.   While the spiritual strength represents God's direct healing power; the shadow is the opposite of the strength, and thus it represents the "absence" of that strength. Finally, the compulsion is a "perversion" of the strength.

Both shadows and compulsions block the power of your spiritual strengths and consequently inhibit your healing. The goal of the SSHP is to activate the power of your spiritual strengths and to diminish the effects of the shadows and the compulsions. (Note: For a more thorough description of the spiritual strengths, the shadows, and the compulsions, see chapter two of Discover Your Spiritual Strengths.)

Pieces of Servant Leadership wisdom are embedded in each of the 90 prayers in this volume: 30 spiritual strengths, 30 shadows, and 30 compulsion prayers. These "wisdom points" are gleaned from many sources, but primarily from the materials and books itemized in the References section at the end of this volume. As you repetitively use these prayers in your onward Servant Leadership development, try to underline these "wisdoms" and incorporate them into your Servant Leader life.

May you always be a strong and striving Servant Leader,

Richard P. Johnson, Ph.D., SSSLC

Gary Ferbet, D.Min.

This prayer book is part of a series of books (see Appendix IV) that all serve to describe and extend the Spiritual Strengths Healing Plan toward one end: to make the program as accessible and as useful to God's children who are dealing with the effects of any sickness, affliction, condition, brokenness, emotional tumult, psychological distress, and/or spiritual dis-ease (that pretty much covers all of us) to find healing. I offer you this program in the hopes that it will bring you new life and new spirit.

What is Servant Leadership?

Servant Leadership is Fundamentally Spiritual Growth

Servant Leadership helps you grow in ways that seem intangible at first, but which can bring immense tangible results over time. Gradually the unseen growth that prayer promotes moves you deeply; it builds humility by allowing you to transcend personal limitations; it's visionary in that you can now find the Spirit in your work; it clears your mind so you can think clearer, it's empathy-producing in that you learn to be authentic; it helps you become God-Reliant, realizing and appreciating your utter dependence on God and on God's power in others…and so much more.

Servant Leadership development focuses on your inner life, and how to use your one-of-a-kind, God-given personality to its best form, indeed Servant Leadership requires changing the ways you use this *"mega-tool"* of your personality (Doohan, 2007). Servant Leadership then is transformative…it makes you "new" by bringing out the most noble parts of you; it helps form you into your "real" you. The prayers in this book can help you activate the best and the most noble parts already in you.

All too often Christian leaders place emphasis for change, development, and growth in the wrong places. Many Christian leaders continue to function with a top-down hierarchical style. Business techniques like strategic planning, goal setting, performance accountability and alignment of the church's vision with the mission plan, and such, consume the energy and time (perhaps too much) of the church's leadership. The results of such a top-down style are, many times, marginal at best. Both staff and volunteers become frustrated because these techniques seem at odds with the inner urges that originally motivated them to serve. Business practices and accounting principles are of course necessary in any organization, faith-based or not; yet when they are over-emphasized they can so saturate the thinking that they can "hijack" the organization and become substitutes for real change—only exercises that fail to generate any lasting change.

Unlike this top-down leadership style, the Servant Leadership concept instead emphasizes collaboration, trust, empathy, and the ethical use of power and influence. At the heart level, the individual is a servant first; he/she makes the conscious decision to lead in order to better serve others, not to accent their own power or security in the system.

Servant Leadership has a multiplying effect within the life of any church or faith-based organization. Servant Leaders promote "owners," not simply laborers, in the church or organization's mission. They create "space" for volunteers and staff to use their creativity and intelligence in defining and addressing challenges. They ask questions to facilitate creative responses rather than to dictate reactions. They do not perceive themselves as experts or "commanders" but with humility and care, they seek to involve others in developing and implementing solutions, directions, and vision. Team building and work engagement improves with successful outcomes.

In contrast, some church leaders, especially those in Senior or Executive (Pastor) roles, can generate diminishing results in the life of the church. Such "diminishers" can take any of a number of behavioral forms: empire builder, egocentric commander, decision-dictator, micromanager, and rescuer. My experience tells me that while such leaders may be well-intentioned, they can perpetrate great damage.

Servant Leaders are "user-friendly" people. Veteran news commentator Tom Brokow spoke of the late Nelson Mandela as a leader and person. Brokow elevated one of Mandela's many attributes when he described him as a "user-friendly" leader. His remark could have meant many things, but for me he made two very important points about Servant Leadership. First, Servant Leaders are approachable to everyone. Secondly, Mandela was someone who loved and cared enough to lead his people into a culture of equality and justice. Servant Leaders are first charged to create a culture of love and care, an environment of compassion and peace. To do so requires a steady reliance on God, not our own understanding. It also requires continuous, bold, and courageous prayer.

Too often within the church or faith-based organization, we place our emphasis on skill sets and the latest trends in organizational ministry rather than who we are as persons and to whom we belong. Skill sets in leadership, management, communication, and strategic planning are helpful in the long run, but they are insufficient for authentic Servant Leadership. Genuine and authentic Servant Leadership comes from "user-friendly" virtues like: humility, mercy, hope, peace, wisdom, empathy, gratitude, harmony, patience, courage and many more. Virtuous Servant Leadership generously allows the intangible presence of the divine into the overall leadership mix.

John Calvin, a seminal thinker of the Reformed tradition, once wrote: "With greater knowledge of one's self, one has greater knowledge of God." While independent studies and workshops on leadership styles and management seminars are helpful in analyzing a leader's position and function in an organization; true leadership begins by accessing the spiritual virtues that God has injected in you. For the Servant Leader then, leadership is a spiritual commitment first and foremost. It is about discerning how

God wants you to use your life in expanding the Kingdom, here and now, with the company of those God has entrusted to your care.

Servant Leadership

While Servant Leadership is a timeless concept, the phrase "Servant Leadership" was coined by Robert K. Greenleaf in "The Servant as Leader," an essay that he first published in 1970. In that essay, Greenleaf said:

> *"The servant-leader is servant first... It begins with the natural feeling that one wants to serve, to serve first. Then conscious choice brings one to aspire to lead. That person is sharply different from one who is leader first, perhaps because of the need to assuage an unusual power drive or to acquire material possessions...The leader-first and the servant-first are two extreme types. Between them there are shadings and blends that are part of the infinite variety of human nature."*

Greenleaf recognized that organizations as well as individuals could be servant-leaders. Indeed, he had great faith that servant-leader organizations could change the world. In his second major essay, "The Institution as Servant" (1972), Greenleaf articulated what is often called the "credo." There he said:

> *"This is my thesis: caring for persons, the more able and the less able serving each other, is the rock upon which a good society is built. Whereas, until recently, caring was largely person to person, now most of it is mediated through institutions – often large, complex, powerful, impersonal; not always competent; sometimes corrupt. If a better society is to be built, one that is more just and more loving, one that provides greater creative opportunity for its people, then the most open course is to raise both the capacity to serve and the*

very performance as servant of existing major institutions by new regenerative forces operating within them."

Most writers see Servant Leadership as an underlying philosophy of leading others, demonstrated through specific characteristics and practices. The foundational concepts are found in Greenleaf's first three major essays, "The Servant as Leader," "The Institution as Servant," and "Trustees as Servants." (NOTE: The Robert Greenleaf Center for Servant Leadership is in Westfield, IN, a suburb of Indianapolis.)

Another Servant Leadership resource: The Center for Servant Leadership at the Pastoral Institute in Columbus, GA, defines Servant Leadership as... *"A lifelong journey that includes discovery of one's self, a desire to serve others, and a commitment to lead. Servant-leaders continually strive to be trustworthy, self-aware, humble, caring, visionary, empowering, relational, competent, good stewards, and community builders."*

Kent Keith, author of *The Case for Servant Leadership*, states that Servant Leadership is ethical, practical, and meaningful. He identifies seven key practices of Servant Leaders: 1) self-awareness, 2) listening, 3) changing the pyramid (from top-down to bottom-up), 4) developing your colleagues, 5) coaching not controlling, 6) unleashing the energy and intelligence of others, and 7) foresight.

James Sipe and Don Frick, in their book *The Seven Pillars of Servant Leadership*, state that servant-leaders are: individuals of character, put people first, are skilled communicators, are compassionate collaborators, use foresight, are systems thinkers, and exercise moral authority.

Unlike leadership approaches with a top-down hierarchical style, Servant Leadership instead emphasizes collaboration, trust, empathy, and the ethical use of power. At heart, the individual is a servant first, making the conscious decision to lead in order to better serve others, not to increase their own power. The objective is to enhance the growth of individuals in the organization and increase teamwork and personal involvement. A recent behavioral economics experiment demonstrates the group benefits of Servant Leadership. Teams of players coordinated their actions better with a Servant Leader resulting in improved outcomes for the followers (but not for the selfless leaders).

Characteristics of Being a Servant Leader

Larry Spears identified ten characteristic of Servant Leaders in the writings of Greenleaf. Leadership experts such as Bolman, Deal, Covey, Fullan, Sergiovanni, and Heifitz also reference these characteristics as essential components of effective leadership.

1. **Listening.** A Servant Leader puts the emphasis upon listening effectively to others.

2. **Empathy.** A Servant Leader needs to understand others' feelings and perspectives.

3. **Healing.** A Servant Leader helps foster each person's emotional and spiritual health and wholeness.

4. **Awareness.** A Servant Leader understands his or her own values and feelings, strengths and weaknesses.

5. **Persuasion.** A Servant Leader influences others through their persuasiveness.

6. **Conceptualizing.** A Servant Leader needs to integrate present realities and future possibilities.

7. **Foresight.** A Servant Leader needs to have a well-developed sense of intuition about how the past, present, and future are connected.

8. **Stewardship.** A Servant Leader is a steward who holds an organization's resources in trust for the greater good.

9. **Commitment to the growth of people.** A Servant Leader is responsible for serving the needs of others.

10. **Building community.** A Servant Leader helps create a sense of community among people.

It must be emphasized that this list of ten characteristics is by no means exhaustive. In addition, the list should not be interpreted as directing any particular manner of behavior in Servant Leaders;

these ten can be expressed in many ways that are unique to the personality of the Servant Leader. Nor is this list a formula to better achieve specific goals; instead they are best conceived as guideposts for walking the journey of Servant Leadership. Each Servant Leader will reflect these ten characteristics differently and in so doing will quite naturally evolve developmentally to what is best in them about Servant Leadership.

Good to Great

In his international blockbuster organizational development book Good to Great, author Jim Collins devotes an entire chapter to Servant Leadership without ever calling it by name. In chapter five, entitled "Level 5 Leadership," Collins adroitly describes the qualities of the style of leadership that turned around companies like Kimberly-Clark, Gillette, Fannie Mae, Rubbermaid, Walgreens, General Electric, and Circuit City. Collins' research team at first intentionally underplayed the role of top management leadership in turning around these and other companies. In the end however, the data screamed at the researchers that the undeniable catalytic agent in every company they studied that achieved sustaining greatness was a leader who exhibited a rare combination of character and style. The list these consummate researchers assembled to describe this unique combination of traits reads like a compacted treatise on Servant Leadership. Their findings included that Level 5 leaders showed:

1. A paradoxical mix of personal humility and unwavering professional will.

2. A compelling modesty...they were self-effacing.

3. Fanatically driven, results-oriented, and possessing of strenuous resolve.

4. Workmanlike diligence.

5. Eagerness to take full responsibility for what may "go wrong."

6. No "personal dazzle," possessed no celebrity leadership, i.e., not at all ego-driven.

7. No boasting; they attributed their success to "good luck."

8. Organizational-motivation...they were not motivated by personal gain.

9. Quiet and calm determination.

10. Modesty, reservation, graciousness, were mild-mannered, under-statement, and self-effacing qualities.

Collins concludes chapter five like this: "Whether or not we make it all the way to Level 5, it is worth the effort. For like all basic truths about what is best in human beings, when we catch a glimpse of that truth, we know that our own lives and all that we touch will be the better for the effort."

Spirituality of Leadership

What, then, are the forces, factors, personal insights and actions that can come together in ways that inject a spiritual dimension into the leadership role? Of the many, many factors that have been itemized and elucidated in the volumes written on leadership, the following six factors may have special impact on up-stepping leadership in the lives of individual leaders, and in the leadership team collectively in ways that generously allow the intangible presence of the divine into the overall leadership mix. This itemization is certainly not exhaustive, but it may serve to stimulate deeper thinking around the nature of leadership in general, and leadership as it is practiced in faith-based organizations particularly.

One: Openness to the Spirit

Spiritual leadership rests primarily on the fundamental belief that the Spirit is present and is active in the lives of those of us who serve as leaders, in those who we serve, and in the process of serving. The function of leading in whatever forum or form it is practiced is animated by the ever-presence of the Spirit. The energy-grace of divinity is accessible; it is real, and it is readily available to those of us who seek it. The process of pursuing this Spirit-power is of course not confined to the leadership role, but is rather one that pervades, even defines, the fullness of all human life. Pursuing the Spirit, and allowing the Spirit to capture us (*Hound of Heaven*, Francis Thompson), involves a lifelong unfolding of our authentic selves, the residence place of the Spirit within us. Indeed, the leadership role is simply another chapter, certainly a vigorously instructive one, in this lifelong unfolding of self-realization...gradually seeing and embracing "the real" in us. Leadership then is a hero's journey of frontally facing the challenges, hardships, frustrations, the many small acceptances, and the huge dilemmas we encounter in the leadership role. Through it all, faithful leaders remain open vessels, ever-ready to receive infusions of grace that offer consolation and engender confidence.

This ever-expanding awareness of the Spirit in the life of a leader multiplies leadership effectiveness beyond the bounds of human direction and onto a numinous plane where leaders come to walk in the solid, stable, and secure mystery of God. Spirit-directed energy (grace) catapults leadership beyond mere human capacity into an arena of faith, the simplicity of knowing and acting in the power of spiritual intangibles that undergird all creation. This jump in human vision, "seeing a higher connection" where human logic and celestial wisdom touch, generates a new synergy and a transformative cohesion into our leadership role that is part of the "newness" of Christ. An inspired leader is ever-aware of the strategic place of the Spirit in the overall vision of the organization, and the tactical hovering of the Spirit in everyday discernment and decisions.

Two: Mission First…Self Only Second

Our leadership is most effective when it is focused primarily on the mission of the organization and only distantly on us as leaders. No leader possesses all the qualities of leadership, nor are the qualities that any one leader possesses ever exercised perfectly. Too often we expect too much of us and of our leadership team; this only brings frustration and contention into our heart and soul, and confusion into the group. The remedy for such, in simplest terms, is a steady and clear focus on what our leadership job calls for, and a personal commitment to do the best we can, knowing that "knocks" will come and need to be absorbed. This virtue speaks to an attitude of perseverance and endurance that can bridge mission and self-sacrifice.

Part of this "mission first…" factor involves cultivating a trusted relationship with a mentor, a confidante with whom we can share frustrations and seek objective clarifications. The guiding hand of a mentor helps us to grow under stress—a valued personal and faith formative enhancement. Developing a relationship with a mentor helps us shed the destructive notion that we can plant our self in our own garden and there become our own vine. Leaders find new life in self-surrender as we come to accept our need for a cleaner abandonment of our ego-self as the director of their personalities, and better separate the "who I am" from the "what I do." Leaders can grow well rounded in the fertility of a healthy mentor relationship; we come to see clearer through the eyes of Christ that we are a branch of the true vine and not the vine itself.

Three: Encourage Always

Spiritual leadership reminds us to train our vision to more readily see the goodness that is resident in all members of our leadership team and in all those we serve as leader. Such self-training is difficult; we need to develop double vision—seeing the tangible reality of whatever situation presents, but also seeing the good that exists within all parties involved. Part of the mission of any faith-based organization is to build a strong community of faith. Too often we focus on "what's wrong"—which appears critical and self-serving rather than mission-serving—rather than on the outworking of the Spirit.

It takes courage to be encouraging. Courage in leadership is about mental and moral strength to venture forth in the face of danger, not in shrinking, fearful, or cowering avoidance. Encouraging others requires determination of character, resolute conviction, and inspirational spunk, without the sting of condescension, presumption, a jaunty hubris. If we are to be encouraging leaders we need to meet strain and stress with fortitude and resilience, not with evasive side-steps, or with headlong, careless, or imprudent action.

Four: Accent Strengths

A strong openness to the Spirit provides us a strong foundation to believe that each person has been endowed with a very special packet of divinity, a reservoir of spiritual strength that defines their soul. This packet of divinity can never be known with certainty, but it can be assumed with confidence. Leadership that builds and uplifts requires that we use a focused spiritual vision to discern strengths and speak to them rather than the shadows that lurk in the darkness of every personality...even our own. Strengths-finding applies to us all. Leadership more grounded in fault-finding in us and others eventually loses suppleness and drains vitality. In order to speak to the strengths of members of their organization, we as leaders need to speak from our "real voice."

To understand "real voice" we need to look at the construct of personality. No one has ever seen a personality, it's a word psychologists made up to refer to the identifiably unique way we express ourselves, or try to. Any personality achieves expression by performing six functions: 1) believing, 2) perceiving, 3) thinking, 4) feeling, 5) deciding, and 6) acting. My research tells me that each one of these personality functions is in turn "powered" by a spiritual strength or virtue (see <u>Discover Your Spiritual Strengths</u>). When we use our personality functions in harmony, when each is aligned with its spiritual strength, then we can speak with our "true voice."

Leaders need to communicate with others, and to communicate well, accurately, compassionately, smoothly, we need to: 1) speak from our spiritual strengths, and 2) speak to the spiritual strengths of others with whom we are communicating. Naturally all of this takes lots of self-understanding and lots of practice; leaders never stop learning how to communicate best, to speak from our spiritual strengths in our true voice and to the spiritual strengths of the person with whom we are communicating. We are most natural, most genuine, most warm, and respectful (and all the rest of good communication) when we access and speak from our spiritual strengths, using this power to say what's truly meaningful to us... so we can say what needs to be said with the greatest possible impact for us personally and for those around us.

Five: Exercise Healthy Letting-Go

We're all reluctant to let go, to let pieces of our past drift into our background. What is especially hard is to let go of former successes that we think somehow define us. We unconsciously feel that our personal identity is resident in these successes. Yet, the process of letting go produces growth and confirms our full presence in our new leadership role. Vestiges of our past can cling to our soul and we let them go only with trepidation that we are giving away our very selves. Such assumptions are illusions that need to be eradicated from our belief core.

The universal need for letting go rests on the virtue of acceptance. Acceptance is not associated with submission or resignation in any way. Rather acceptance is honoring the sense of being in accord with God; it means giving God one's complete "amen," it means seeking alignment between our own will and God's will, and letting go in trust. Acceptance is from Love and Love is about growth.

Six: Make Prayer Your Priority

As leaders we are called to consistent, even constant prayer. This call is especially acute in times of trial when we need to be as open as possible to the inspiring power of God's grace. Prayer adds to the efficacy of leadership in many ways. Prayer has the power to transform us—making us more resilient to the barrage of discomfort that leadership can sometimes bring. Prayer is a mighty force for promoting and sustaining our own health and well-being. Prayer, due to its introspective nature, is a sound psychological process as well as a spiritually uplifting one. Prayer allows the leader to come to a fuller realization of his own God-given powers and to focus them more clearly and precisely.

Prayer brings us into more intimate and conscious contact with God, and opens us up to God's healing power of grace. Prayer positions the leader to receive the maximum benefit from the abundant treasure of healing grace that God provides for him every day. Prayer mends spiritual afflictions and moral infirmities. Prayer re-energizes a heart grown limp, a mind grown dim and lazy, and a spirit grown uninspired. Prayer motivates, both psychologically and spiritually, so that the leader's best giftedness if brought forward into the light.

No leader possesses all six of these qualities of leadership, neither are the qualities he does possesses ever exercised perfectly. The key is to know what the job of leadership calls for and to try to do our very best (sounds trite but it's profoundly true). Fully ingesting and accepting this truism constitutes a turning point in the ongoing process of leadership as a personal growth imperative.

"Stay focused on the mission...not on oneself!"

~ Stephen Tutas, Servant Leader

Daily Prayers for Servant Leaders in Churches and Faith-Based Organizations

by

Richard P. Johnson, Ph.D.

&

Gary H. Ferbet, D.Min.

Section One

The Believing Function

The Believing Function

These five spiritual strengths are the love-energy, or grace, that allows you to believe clearly, accurately, "rightly," and thereby position you to best bring healing (through God's grace) to your life and leadership.

One of these five strengths is your premier spiritual strength (as identified by your personal SSHP), which means that, for whatever reason, this spiritual strength is the most prominent, the most powerful for you at this time. You do have the other four in your personality, but at this time in your life they are of somewhat lessened power than your premier spiritual strength. Under each spiritual strength you will find its shadow, (the absence of the strength), and its compulsion (or perversion of the strength).

Morning Prayer

God-Reliance

Lord you are the beginning and the end of my life, the Alpha and the Omega.

God, you are the fountain of all goodness, all virtue, and all energy.

Today I seek to capture the fullness of your gift of God-Reliance as my fundamental source of Servant Leadership power. It is the strength of God-Reliance that affords me the self-agency so necessary for Servant Leadership.

You are the beginning and the end of my life, the Alpha and the Omega.

You are the rock upon which I can rely in all disturbing times.

I want dearly to believe entirely and thoroughly in you, to see with your eyes, think with your mind, feel with your heart, choose with your will, and act with your hands.

I center the entire value system of my belief core on you and around you. Now, more than ever, I need your strength to find union with you.

By your omnipotent energy of love, I find the power and might to always seek solidarity with you.

I do not simply *believe* in you, dear Lord. I *know* in you. I am utterly convicted of your active role in my life in general and in my Servant Leadership role in particular.

I seek your help in sustaining my complete reliance on you as the indomitable foundation of my being, the cornerstone which you have planted in me from time immemorial.

Amen

Afternoon Prayer

Doubt

The Shadow of God-Reliance

Help me overcome my doubt, my skepticism, and my uncertainty.

Lord, I seek release from the turmoil and torture of any remnants of the shadow of doubt.

With your grace, help me lighten the burden of my questioning mind that leads me to dispute what I know is right.

You are the first source and center of the cosmos; you are the creator of all and the primal force that sustains me and everything in this world.

You are the only source of love, and love is the singular source of all that is real in the universe.

Help me overcome whatever distrust, skepticism, or uncertainty that may haunt me.

Sustain me through my periods of unbelief, and carry me beyond my need to control the uncontrollable.

Be with me Lord when I falter in my belief. Doubt pushes me into a belief that I'm missing that deeper connection with my ministry, your Spirit in my work, which I need for true Servant Leadership.

Be my rock of security when I stray and lose sight of my core conviction that you are everything.

Save me from my tendencies to rush to judgment, a place within me where I only suffer from self-imposed isolation.

Amen

Evening Prayer

Dependency

The Compulsion of God-Reliance

*I have many dependencies, yet all of them are unreal,
except my need for you, Lord.*

Lord, I pray that you offer me the power of God-Reliance to reduce my excessive needs.

I need only you, because you are the foundation of my soul, the rock of my security.

All my supposed needs are but artificial facsimiles of my one and only need...You!

I'm so tempted to see my value only in terms of those around me, or in my achievements.

I have developed many dependencies, and all of them are unreal, except my need for you, dear Lord.

When I subordinate my spirit to the desires of others and not your desires, Lord, I revert to a regressive attitudinal default position which blocks you from animating enlightened faith-based leadership in me.

Help me gain confidence in you, Lord, so I can stop giving my decisions away to the swings and sways of the world.

I know that you are my only rock, you are my only surety, and you are my only certainty, dear Lord.

Help me "be" in you, and believe completely in you, always.

Amen

Morning Prayer

Humility

*Today I am free from confusion about who I am,
because I now know who I am.*

Good morning, Lord. Today I dedicate myself to <u>do</u> and to <u>be</u> your will.

Today I seek to be nothing other than what I authentically am.

Humility calls me to be real, to claim my hurts but also to claim my strengths equally.

Help me not forget that I am gifted, and that your gifts in me need to be exercised, lest I lose them.

Humility calls me to be true to myself, my True Self, not the facsimile ego self that sometimes masquerades around as me.

I am first and foremost your child, dear Lord; all else is meager and transitory, only time-limited roles I play here on this plane.

Only you define my real self, Lord, which of course is your presence in me. Humility calls me to honor that real self as the only true definition of me.

I am in this world to discover the truest reality of me, the love you have invested in me, in relationship with you.

Today, in the name of humility, I will take off any masks that I've been wearing, and take down any facades that I may have constructed that prevent me from recognizing and transcending any leadership failures that may now prove instructive for me.

In this way I am free from worry and confusion about who I am, because I now know who I am.

Amen

Afternoon Prayer

Self-Centeredness

The Shadow of Humility

Dear Lord, allow me to "own" my own truth, which is your truth within me.

Save me, dear Lord, from my ferocious need to puff myself up, to be different from the truth of who I am.

Spare me, through your gift of humility, so I can turn away from my desires to be other than what and who I am.

Let your humility pull me toward your authenticity and toward my own, as I come to more fully understand that the common good is a more important leadership goal than is my own self-achievement.

Help me avoid my vulnerability to model myself after what the world sees as beautiful, or sexy, or strong, or powerful, or trendy, or any other illusion.

Help me model myself after you alone, Lord.

Dear Lord, allow me to "own" my own truth, which is actually your truth within me, and not indulge in self-love above loving you.

I know that your strength can foil my conceit, eradicate my complacency, and defuse my exaggerated sense of self-importance.

Help me see beyond my terrible tendency toward selfishness.

Amen

Evening Prayer

Self-Abasement

The Compulsion of Humility

Self-abasement closes me off from my own true reality.

Dear Lord, grant me a stronger grip on your strength of humility in me so I can get out from under the burdensome weight of fearing the scrutiny of others.

I know that humility releases me from my compulsion of self-abasement; true humility rolls away the heavy stones of inferiority, shame, and guilt that I've been carrying far too long.

Humility offers me the grace to be authentic in how I present myself, so I can better learn who I genuinely am, and to adopt my most real leadership style.

Self-abasement closes me off from my own true reality.

Your humility in me allows me to know the rightness of my own convictions and frees me from always believing that the thoughts of others are better than my own.

I so want and need your grace to emancipate me from my lack of faith in the strengths that you have already given me; help me capture your grace, dear Lord.

I no longer wish to neglect myself by overlooking your promise of love.

I know that I can begin to believe in the true me like I never have before.

Amen

Morning Prayer

Acceptance

Today I offer you my complete "Amen."

Oh, what a happy day it is, knowing that you are with me, Lord.

Today my only goal is to live in your love, to be in your holy strength of acceptance.

I aspire to be nothing less than your sacred acceptance today.

Lord, I long to live in perfect accord with only you.

I seek only to align my truth with yours.

Today I offer you my complete "amen."

I utter the words of holy acceptance, not as resignation or submission but as the true spiritual "grit" that affirms me as the "me" that you desire.

Today I know your authority over me is a holy act of kindness that fully knows what and who I am, and only desires that I live in your abundance.

Help me to fully accept your plan for my life and aspire to live it out as best I can today.

Lord, help me accept the "who" of me, and also the "what" of me so they can align together into a Servant Leadership style that best reflects the fullness of you in me.

Amen

Afternoon Prayer

Dissension

The Shadow of Acceptance

I seek only to flow with your holy currents of grace and not against them.

Dear Lord, lift the terrible weight of dissension from me.

I wander away from you every time I disagree with your gentle direction, every time I turn away in unexamined resistance.

I want to accept your will, Lord, and not continuously fight what I know without question is good for me.

Help me shake my adolescent need to sometimes feel at odds with others and with your desires for me.

I seek only to flow with, not against, your holy currents of grace as my shadow of dissension lures me to do.

Lord, help me embrace any dissension within me as a master teacher of the art of acceptance, and so weave the ultimate acceptance factor of respecting myself and others into the fabric of my leadership efforts.

Keep me from hostility of any kind, against others or against myself; and most of all, keep me from being indifferent to you, dear Lord.

Help me to stay aligned with you and not at variance from you.

Help me stop fighting all those paper dragons of my own making, Lord.

Amen

Evening Prayer

Aloofness

The Compulsion of Acceptance

*Help me to connect rather than detach from others,
myself, and you.*

Stir me up, dear Lord, so that I can rest in the warm love of you, and not distance myself from you in some chilly and dispassionate avoidance.

Being cool makes my life a bit colder, as well as aloof from others around me.

Help me to connect rather than detach from others, and from myself.

Sometimes I fear that I inadvertently push away sustained and close interaction, and so I unknowingly protect myself from imagined harm by giving others a cold shoulder of aloofness.

Break me of my habit to remove myself, and keep me united with others instead of feeling the defensive need to "fly solo."

But Lord, my most terrible aloofness is when I distance myself from you, when I absurdly believe that I can "go it alone" without you, or even confuse myself into believing that my will is somehow better than yours!

Being aloof frustrates constructive change, the goal of enlightened Servant Leadership; while acceptance calls me to adopt "right attitudes" for positive change.

Amen

Morning Prayer

Mercy

Help me extend my hand as your hand to others today, Lord.

As the sun breaks through and warms the earth this morning, by your grace I reassert my conviction that mercy is the essential power in my life today, Lord.

I seek compassion, forbearance, and tenderness toward others and myself in your grace of mercy.

Help me extend my hand to others as your hand—offering them the fullness of your power and presence.

Today I seek to recognize and practice mercy everywhere: from humanitarian giving to empathic listening, and from leniency to true pity.

Motivate me to see the plight of others and act to soothe their pain only in your Spirit.

Help me fill my being and saturate my entire personality with your mercy.

Dear Lord, help me be humane and just today. As your power of mercy is tender and caring it also helps me assist my organization in ways so it can grow toward becoming a leadership-nurturing organization.

Grant me your strength of forgiving mercy.

I long to "be" your mercy to myself and to others today, dear Lord.

Amen

Afternoon Prayer

Indifference

The Shadow of Mercy

Release me from the demon of indifference; only your grace can save me.

Lord, help me remove the fangs from the shadow of indifference.

Let me be attentive not bored, decisive not lack-luster, active in you not lazy, vital not careless.

Lord, please cleanse me of my terrible indifference that blocks your hand from touching mine.

Help me surmount the leadership laziness of indifference, the force of neglect that disables my values and causes me to overlook the mission, the purpose, and the forward direction of my organization.

Indifference pushes me away from those in need, and it lures me to a defensive criticism of those who most require help.

Indifference keeps me silent when I could say a kind word; a word of additive clarification or consolation; indifference stops me from caring, and it hardens my heart.

I seek release from this demon, Lord; only your grace can save me.

I need your consoling hand to awaken me from the somnolence of indifference.

Make me uncomfortable with myself when I'm tempted to turn a blind eye, or when I criticize rather than be moved by true pity.

Give me the strength of mercy to overcome my oppressive indifference.

Amen

Evening Prayer

Legalism

The Compulsion of Mercy

I can, at times, be stubborn and stiff-necked, demanding, and excessively strict.

Lord, I seek your grace to extract me from the pit of over-reliance on standards and rules, regulations, and laws as the primary authority of my life.

I know that you are the only authority, but too often, out of fear, I can over-invest in the authority of human experts and/or cultural standards as my primary guiding principles for living.

I falter when I fall victim to our worldly media that overlooks the authenticity of your teaching.

Save me from the confusion of legalism, dear Lord.

I sometimes hold myself and others to overly strict "rules" of thinking and behavior; I demand that others conform to my beliefs; I negate their thinking by not truly listening to them.

I can, at times, be stubborn and stiff-necked, demanding, and excessively strict. Save me in these times of trial.

Save me from imposing this loathsome legalism on everything: others, institutions, the Church, people in authority, on myself, and also on you, dear Lord.

Legalism confounds the leadership resilience of mercy to forge ahead and address those hard questions of what most needs doing in the organization right now.

Amen

Morning Prayer

Hope

The splendor of the virtue of hope lights my way and leads me to you today.

God, I know that you are the architect of my soul.

You chose to place the power of hope in me, and I know that you expect me to be a channel of your hope for the world.

I know that I am most happy, healthy, and holy when I'm in love with you in hope.

Let me greet this day with the enthusiasm and optimism that flows only from your hope.

Help me always respond in your hope and not react with my shadow of despair or my compulsive of presumption.

The virtue of hope is that generous grace of leadership that, among other things, gives me the power to remain open to the potentials and possibilities in myself, those on my Servant Leadership team, and in all those I serve.

The splendor of hope lights my way and leads me to you today, Lord.

Propelled by your gift of hope, I have absolute assurance that your power of love can never be eclipsed; there is no power in the universe stronger than your love.

I have a deep conviction that your love will always remain the compelling power in the cosmos.

Amen

Afternoon Prayer

Despair

The Shadow of Hope

I always need your hope to regain my bearings and find the center of my soul.

The realization that I have strayed from your gift of hope startles and shakes me, dear Lord.

I can find myself slipping toward despair in so many ways.

I need, always need, your hope to regain my bearings and find the center of my soul.

Dear Lord, you know that I can become irritable, disillusioned, and even dreary and flat at times.

Grant me your hope, Lord, especially when I shirk away from hope and feel sad, melancholy, and weary.

I can sometimes even feel empty, fatigued, and guilty. In those times, grant me your hope, Lord.

Despair strips me of purpose. I can't answer the central question of purpose, "Why are we here?" I can't align my personal purpose with organizational purpose; despair confuses my leadership value.

Grant me your hope, Lord; spare me from sliding all the way from you, with my back to the wall in abject hopelessness.

This is not the real me and certainly this is not what you want for me.

Activate my hope Lord, and save me from the sting of dismay and the abyss of despair.

Amen

Evening Prayer

Presumption

The Compulsion of Hope

Save me from thinking that I can somehow save myself.

Lord, I don't know that I'm moving toward presumption until I actually get there.

Help me recognize when I'm slipping; help me access your hope to catch me, at least to become more aware that I'm moving in that direction.

Lord, help me surmount my vulnerability of taking things for granted.

Help me temper my tendency to "know it all" or to think that my thoughts and ideas are simply "better."

Help me resist taking liberties that are not mine to take.

I can take undeserved credit for "my" accomplishments when actually you, not me, are the engineer and prime mover.

I seem to have a built-in belief that I'm entitled to favored treatment above others, which only blocks my growth and healing.

Save me from believing that I can somehow save myself; that somehow my "successes" come from my own work and not from you.

Dear Lord, help me believe in the real me and not the presumed me; and in that conversion, help me discover a clearer reality.

Presumption hijacks the leadership spiritual strength of hope and contorts it into the pursuit of personal gain rather than in its rightful cause…advancing the common good of the organization and your glory.

Amen

Section Two

The Perceiving Function

The Perceiving Function

Only rarely are you aware of your <u>awareness</u>. Your outlook on the world and your <u>insight</u> into yourself is accomplished, for the most part, without the slightest <u>recognition</u> of what you're doing. Perceptions just seem to happen without any intention or volition on your part, yet how you <u>frame or imagine</u> what you encounter directs your personal and professional life. What you choose to <u>focus</u> upon, and how you choose to frame it becomes your world; your perceptions make the world in which you live your reality!

Your premier perceiving spiritual strength draws you toward the truth, while the shadow and compulsion of your perceiving premier strength pulls you toward unreality. It's only in reality where you can find your true voice, your path to optimal functioning. Your over-arching of your Servant Leadership, building up the Kingdom of God, calls you to an awareness of that which is beyond the material plane. Your inner calling beckons you to stretch to a farther horizon of awareness, to see the divinity that is the driving force of your personality (page 95, <u>Discover Your Spiritual Strengths: Find Health, Healing & Happiness).</u>

Morning Prayer

Leadership Vision

I can catch a glimpse of the eternal, a reflection of heaven right here.

This morning I awaken from my sleepiness to discover a new world of color and detail, of enhanced hue and brightness, a newness of which I was previously unaware.

Today I can sense your presence keener, dear Lord, as I see through the powerful lens of the strength of your vision.

I know, from the depth of my core, that you offer me pearls of light that contain the power to lift my Servant Leadership role beyond the mundane.

Your grace of vision in me allows me to see clearly what the organization does and why it does it—vision gives me the horizon of meaning that would otherwise elude me. I am blessed with your vision Lord.

I see things with ever-finer clarity as I grow closer to you. You do indeed make all things new, dear Lord.

Vision allows me to see a reflection of your face just beyond the material world.

Today I sense your presence anew; and in my mind's eye, I imagine you everywhere.

It's as though I can catch a glimpse of the eternal, a reflection of heaven, right here…right now. I literally see things differently; I see your hand in everything, everywhere, and in everyone.

Lord, help me stay centered in your vision all day long.

Amen

Afternoon Prayer

Blindedness

The Shadow of Vision

Help me focus on what is of you, Lord, and away from what is not.

Oh how I wish release from the shadow of blindedness.

Help me Lord, open my eyes and sharpen all my senses so I don't fall into "seeing darkly" today. Help me reflect on my own perceptions as I lead others by taking my lead from you.

Enhance my limited perception and enrich my imagination so I can see your points of light inside me overtaking any darkness there.

Blindedness makes me insecure and clumsy; it causes me to stumble over the same nothingness that I stumbled over yesterday, and yesterday, and the yesterday before that.

Help me focus on what is of you, Lord, and away from what is not.

Take the logs from my eyes that distort my vision and deaden my soul.

Help me search only for what is real.

Let me see with your eyes, Lord, so that I can once again see clearly.

Through the marvelous mystery of your grace, help me find you, and there discover the power to successfully deal with change and the energy to help those I serve graduate to a larger vision of what's possible.

Amen

Evening Prayer

Illusion

The Compulsion of Vision

Shift my point of view so I can perceive "rightly."

Why do I make real what is not, Lord?

Why do I focus on things of the world like contention, jealousy, shame, anger, twisted motivation, arrogance, distrust, fear, and the like when I want so much to focus on the real truth which is only of you?

Help my distorted vision see what is real and distinguish it from what is mere illusion. Shift my point of view so I can perceive "rightly."

I seek the true meaning of things and not some facsimile that is but an illusion of truth.

Help me see through your lens of life so I can see clearly, not darkly.

Lord, help me see all the case-in-point lessons of leadership that you present to me every day. Let me recognize these as teachers—there to instruct me on the finer points of leadership in your name.

When I see my foibles only as terrorists attacking me, then I'm in illusion and don't see the teacher that resides there.

Help me to see through the illusions of the world and view all of your creation as essentially good and not fearsome.

I know that you wish that I live my life in abundance, and seeing accurately is a step toward that abundance.

Amen

Morning Prayer

Humor

I can almost see God smiling at me.

Today I awaken to my authentic self; that place in me where the Spirit resides, and I smile broadly because I recognize how silly I can be sometimes.

I'm moved to laugh at my foibles, quirks, and inconsistencies of thought and behavior.

When I see myself clearly I recognize how laughable some of my behaviors really are. Let my leadership value grow in the sacred light of a light-hearted but purposeful humor.

If I don't find humor in these personal idiosyncrasies, then I only find self-condemnation.

I chuckle at myself when I come to appreciate the view of me as I think you see me: you don't look at me with an eye for what's wrong, rather, you only see what's right, and good, and precious.

I can almost see you smiling at me right now—just as a mother might smile at her child's mistake, or find comical a bit of "cute" behavior.

Lord, continue the flow of your grace of humor so I can see all of me, and especially Lord, grant me the vision to learn the best of your leadership style that arrays itself right in front of me every day.

Let your light of humor push away all in me that is not of you.

Amen

Afternoon Prayer

Lamentation

The Shadow of Humor

Strengthen me with holy humor, your grace that opens me beyond lamentation.

Save me from the different forms of woe that I perpetrate on myself, Lord.

Bless me with your grace—that point of light called humor that you placed within me.

Help me recognize when I'm inching away from humor and over to the shadow of lamentation.

Help turn me around and away from self-pity, away from whining and grumbling, and away from complaint and criticism.

Grant me a new view of loss and disappointments so I don't become trapped in a vortex of leadership helplessness.

Awaken me to your sacred illumination that soothes and even heals me of the terrible woes of hopelessness that threaten to overtake me at times.

Strengthen me with holy humor, your celestial grace that opens me beyond the confines of lamentation. Help me see the humor in my foibles and experience the full power of your care in me.

Lord, when it's necessary, help me see the value of letting go of even those things that I worked so hard to achieve in the past so they do not entrap my leadership today. I seek to be free to carry on with renewed purpose.

Amen

Evening Prayer

Recklessness

The Compulsion of Humor

*Let me not poke fun at others, belittle, or mock them
with a vicious chuckle or smirk.*

Oh Lord, help me surmount my vulnerability toward recklessness, that
terrible compulsion that perverts your beautiful gift of humor into an
underhanded means of gaining false stature.

I can use recklessness to cut others down by making fun of them. I can
sometimes cover over my own errors with a "humorous" quip designed
to side-step personal accountability.

Let me see clearer how recklessness might be pushing me to make a joke
at other's expense, or by "teasing" them to elevate myself, or even
folding a half-disguised insult into a "light-hearted" comment.

Let your true humor in me shine through all such situations reflecting
your perfection through me.

And Lord, let me not avoid your call to true leadership by engaging in
clever jokes or crafty and deceiving comments meant only to divert
attention away from those things that need focus, attention, and action
now.

Lord, help me use your humor to gain a new and steady orientation and a
sustaining reassurance, so I don't fall into sarcasm that only serves to
divide me, confuse those I lead, and confound my leadership.

Amen

Morning Prayer

P e a c e

I see the world clearer as I look through the lens of your peace.

Gracious Lord, I know that you've been watching over me the whole night through, and now your calm eyes greet me as I open mine to this day.

I see the world clearer as I look through the lens of your peace, and feel your celestial quiet saturating my heart with a sure calmness that only comes from you.

Harmony rests gently on me as your sacred tranquility innervates every crevice, fold, and juncture of my being.

Lord, help me experience your peace as we continue traveling on our mysterious and wonderful journey together today.

You are love itself, and I seek to live and serve in that love.

Your peace is a portion of that love, Lord, and so I strive to seek out your peace today.

I needn't look far because you have tenderly planted your peace right in me; it purposefully patrols my being as a point of light seeking only to hold me up.

Lord, grant me the leadership peace to help my people gain a quiet sense of community working in this organization; a sense of belonging, rather than coming here each day to simply perform job functions.

Help me find peace today, Lord, and remain in it all day long.

Amen

Afternoon Prayer

Contention

The Shadow of Peace

Transform any of my oppositional tendencies into instruments for peace.

Oh Lord, my brokenness pushes me toward contention much too often.

Help me move to peace when I'm tempted to be defensive, or upset, or cold, or contrary.

I don't wish these divisive reactions, Lord; of course I don't; nonetheless, they show up in my life just the same, driven by the murky inner shadow force of contention.

Your peace is the center of my soul and it's from this base of peace, this center point light of peace, that I seek an enlightened leadership that is not about holding onto "my ground," but is more about leading others to new territory; a higher ground that perhaps only a few can see as beneficial for the common good, but which is necessary for peace to grow.

Lord, offer me the grace to convert any anger in me into a force for good and not become distorted in destruction.

Transform any of my oppositional tendencies into instruments of peace.

Lift any hint of defensiveness from me so I can see better who I am, and the fact that the real me needs no protection.

Help me, Lord, to grow beyond provoking contention in others or within myself, and instead always sow peace.

Amen

Evening Prayer

Appeasement

The Compulsion of Peace

Save me from placating or pacifying others, fooling myself, and losing your peace.

Lord, save me from making a "false peace" within my heart.

Help me make the best use of my experience and not cave in only to "look good" by giving unreasonable and unnecessary concessions. This is not leadership; it's not the voice of my strengths, but only that of my insecurity.

Let me dig into the depths of your peace where I know I will find the motivation to see clearly in your wholeness that resides there.

Help me shoulder the responsibility of making a true peace within me, with those around me, and with all my disappointments and hurts as well.

Let me not falsely apologize or over-promise; save me from excessive explanations and/or painful back-peddling.

Save me from placating or pacifying others and fooling myself; all of this only generates the false peace of appeasement.

Let me never abandon my true needs of moving only toward you.

Being a reflection of you, Lord, is my only goal...my only quest in living.

Light up my leadership with your grace, so I can see what needs to be done in the brightness of your peace.

Amen

Morning Prayer

Adaptability

Adaptability is essential for spiritual growth, without it I am doomed to remain the same.

How wonderful to awaken and view the world this morning in the new light of adaptability.

I luxuriate knowing that not only can I change, but also that you, Lord, expect me to change.

My only job today, as it is every day, is to learn how to love better than I did yesterday.

Learning how to love better requires your adaptability, Lord. I am empowered by your gift of adaptability that allows me to shift my view as I grow in love.

Adaptability is essential for spiritual growth, without it I am doomed to the whims of my foibles. Lord, you want and expect the opposite for and from me.

Adaptability propels me to see the light of your ways operating in me, and so not to blindly take on the ways of the world.

I can learn your will by seeing the abundance that has been invested in me.

I can adjust myself toward you, Lord, I can be malleable in your hands; I can bend toward your ways and away from the ways of the world.

Lord, you call me to shift the ways I use the tool of my personality. Help me shift gears smoothly so I can lead with new resolve and leave behind tired and worn out ways. Help me find ways of leading my people closer to you, closer to optimal and authentic functioning.

Amen

Afternoon Prayer

Rigidity

The Shadow of Adaptability

Lord, I long to see through your eyes of compassion, understanding, trust, and genuineness.

Lord, save me from the rigidity of sameness; save me from the threat of spiritual monotony.

You are alive in me and you call my deepest self to you. I cannot be the same as I was yesterday and still grow toward you.

Sometimes I need to change my perspective and shift my point of view, so I can better align with yours.

Help me not cast a critical eye toward your creation, and help me get past my first tendencies to analyze and evaluate; instead, help me first experience your splendor in everything.

Lord, I long to see through your eyes of compassion, understanding, trust, and genuineness.

For all this, I lay myself at the feet of your grace of adaptability.

Help me take the logs out of my eyes and see my position of leadership as a change-agent, a means to grow closer to you, to see your splendor and hear your music so I can be all that your adaptability in me calls me to be, and grow closer to that call.

Save me from stagnation and immobility and from being overly strict or harsh in my view of others and myself.

Amen

Evening Prayer

Self-Forfeiture

The Compulsion of Adaptability

Adaptability is my light this evening, the light of grace that illuminates me.

Oh happy evening! The shadows grow longer and I'm reminded of your magnificent gift of holy adaptability.

In its light, I can view my own needs as equally important to the needs of others.

I do have the ability to say "no" to unnecessary tasks and demands.

Let me not forget that I possess a sense of direction. I see that I am able to lead closer to my true self only in you, Lord.

Help me not to be tempted or sidetracked by the idle cares and pseudo-needs of my ego or of others. My views are valuable and I need to learn better how to express them in humility.

Adaptability is my light this evening, the point of light of grace that illuminates every corner of me with your power so I can show the parts of you in me, and express my real self, the truth of me in the ways and means of your call to Servant Leadership.

Sacred adaptability teaches me to discern and to trust my true perspective as a facet of your love, dear Lord.

I retain my integrity, my wholeness of spirit, by holding onto my true self, the packet of divinity you have planted in me.

Amen

Morning Prayer

Simplicity

I fully recognize the hand of God.

I marvel at the beauty of the morning light gracing the edge of my bed.

Today I awaken in exquisite sensitivity, like an infant touching her mother.

I see the morning light as beams of grace from above; I am enthralled by its majesty.

Help me be fully present and comprehend what's really happening in any situation today so I can take the necessary adaptive leadership steps.

I depend on your light, Lord, so I can better read the simple truth of the experience of this day. Let me see and appreciate the exquisite grandeur of this day as it dawns by your hand.

Today is sweet, uncomplicated, innocent, and without pretense—as am I also at my true core of grace.

Today is good; it possesses that divine quality of God that knows no bounds.

I experience this goodness and likewise know no boundaries today in appreciating the beautiful simplicity of the moment I now savor and want to keep in my heart all day long.

In true Servant Leadership, help me be present to those you have entrusted to me. Help me be available and respond to problems and concerns with a simple smile.

Amen

Afternoon Prayer

Complexity

The Shadow of Simplicity

Let my vision not be clouded by data and details that only serve to obscure your reality.

God, save me from my shadow of complexity.

Let the point of light that is your grace of simplicity illuminate away that terrible darkness of complexity within me that bends my perception into distortion and stirs up fear in me.

Help me remain vigilantly watchful for any overload or pressure that may upend my internal balance of grace.

Let my leadership vision not be clouded by excessive data and walls of details that only serve to obscure your reality, Lord, and confound the simplicity I know to be true.

Save me from undue complications or entanglements that lure me toward the siren's song of complexity.

Lord, bring my hurts into the light of this day with its simple, childlike cheer; a cheer that you asked me to adopt as a sign of your love.

Save me from the paralysis that comes from excessive complexity, and grant me your simple yet profound ways of peace today.

As a Servant Leader, help me deal with the advancing complexity from the "new commons." Give me the creative insight into the needs of my people as we all deal with the demands of the marketplace.

Amen

Evening Prayer

Bluntedness

The Compulsion of Simplicity

I can become insensitive to the needs of others and blind to my own needs as well.

Without warning or awareness I can too often pervert my wondrous gift of simplicity and move toward bluntedness.

In this dark place, I can further slip into an oversimplification that perverts my thinking away from your truth and toward an excessively narrow assessment of reality that can be far from the truth.

Help me remain in the simple truth of advancing complexity and not be overwhelmed by it to the point of toxic interactions with those I lead.

In this confined state I don't see the fullness of reality. I can become critical rather than appreciative, obtuse rather than approachable, and tactless rather than respectfully genuine. I can too easily overlook the needs of others and blind to my own needs as well.

I can judge others and myself, heaping on them underserved ridicule and even prejudicial comments, which only blocks the flow of grace and blunts my leadership tools: being vulnerable, expressing honest feelings, remaining open to doubts, and admitting my mistakes and failures.

Help me see a new day in a new way, a day when I can honor the simple truth without distorting it into something unreal.

Lord, help me replace irreverence with respect and harsh views with your simple and beautiful ones.

Amen

Section Three

The Thinking Function

The Thinking Function

Thoughts are your almost automatic internal communications; they're like hundreds or maybe even thousands of internal e-mails flying around your mind at the same time—each carrying bits of data. Some of these e-mails come from your perceiving function and contain data from the outside world; others are internally produced by your thinking function. Through all this, it's hard to make sense of what's really going on and how to make sense of it. We need a filter.

You are thinking all the time, and the vast majority of that time you're quite unaware of what you're thinking. All these ideas are racing around your mind, each one charged with energy, and you're oblivious to them. Servant Leadership calls you to become more aware of your thoughts: the ones that help you and the ones that don't (page 121, <u>Discover Your Spiritual Strengths: Find Health, Healing & Happiness</u>).

Morning Prayer

Faith

In the debris of my thoughts, I find solace on the solid rock of the grace of faith.

Something heavy pulls at my heart this morning as I raise my head off my pillow.

This unnamed intruder tugs at my mood dragging it down. Where it came from is a mystery.

Amongst the debris of my fragmented thoughts, I find solace only on the solid rock of the grace of faith.

It's here in this place of fidelity where I know without question that your guiding hand brings me back to my center.

It's here where I stand on holy ground; knowing this settles my irritated mind and calms my thoughts.

You are my loyalty, dear Lord; you are my conviction; in you I find rest.

My brokenness, whatever it is, cannot overcome my faith; but paradoxically it can strengthen my faith if I get out of the way and let your healing hands work, Lord.

The light of your grace of faith penetrates deep into every part of me, searching out any of my broken thoughts and replacing them with firmness and confidence.

Leadership development is, at its base, spiritual growth…faith in your faith. Help me remain faithful to you, Lord, in all facets of my personal and professional life.

Amen

Afternoon Prayer

Disloyalty

The Shadow of Faith

Pour out your grace of faith; illuminate my mind so I can think clearly again.

Oh, how my thoughts can twist my mind and cause me to resist you, Lord.

Help me live by your precepts; help me align my thoughts with yours; help me bend my knee as your faithful servant, as you are so mystifyingly a servant for me.

Give me the grace of faith to collect my scattered thoughts, which divide and confuse my mind, pulling it away from you.

Help me bring my thoughts back to you.

As a Servant Leader, I aspire to exercise loyalty to you, Lord, and all that flows from you. This leadership loyalty is always concerned with and is directed toward the genuine common good of the organization. Help me convert myself to that common good, which is essentially your good.

Pour out your grace of faith; illuminate my mind so I can think clearly and accurately.

Enlighten my thinking so I can remain loyal to you and your teaching.

Extend to me, Lord, the grace of loyalty, the source of which is the only power strong enough to overcome my mistakes and missteps.

Help me find obedience so I can use your light of grace to overcome the darkness of my hurts and then discover your healing hand already on me.

Amen

Evening Prayer

Over-Zealousness

The Compulsion of Faith

Help me, Lord, to stay centered in you so that I don't get "carried-away" with thoughts.

Dear Lord, help me tap into your strength so I can shift my near-obsessive thoughts back to you.

I seem unable to rid my mind of meaningless and self-centered thoughts that futilely focus on changing other people, the world, me, and even you, Lord. I don't want compulsive thoughts; I want to be single-minded about you alone.

Help me, Lord, stay centered in and on you so that I don't get "carried-away" with my thoughts about changing what is unchangeable at this time.

I am convicted about my thinking, but at times my conviction can extend beyond the borders of reason.

In a sense, I lose control of my thinking; my thinking begins controlling me rather than me controlling it.

Help me find your true faith, dear Lord, and in this power from you I know I will discover the most accurate direction for all my leadership tasks. This requires that I recognize a new mode of operating from within…consulting with and speaking from the voice of my spiritual strengths.

Help me center on the point of light of faith that you have planted in me from my conception.

Amen

Morning Prayer

Wisdom

Let me join my mind with your mind, dear Lord.

Dear Lord, animate me with your wisdom all day long. Saturate my thoughts with your highest purpose so I can lead with confidence.

Allow me to let go of all unnecessary thoughts that only clutter my mind and bring it to insufficiency.

Let me use the knowledge that flows from you as the basis for my thinking all day, Lord.

Let me discover and use the most illuminated, enlightened, enriching thoughts…your thoughts, so that I can discern the "right meaning" from the events and relationships of this day.

Let me join my mind with your mind, so that I can find your uplifting unity of thought that gives me confidence, good cheer, and the necessary depth to bring your wisdom to the table.

Let me properly discern your wisdom in ways that allow me to walk straight and solid with you all day long.

Help me embrace your light, overcome my dread of darkness, and find my healing path to you.

Grant me your wisdom so I can read the larger patterns operating in my organization and be the best leader I can be. Help me discern the best and the most efficacious meaning from every person and every situation I encounter.

Amen

Afternoon Prayer

Inadequacy

The Shadow of Wisdom

Clear away my cloudy and folly-filled thinking.

Dear Lord, allow the brightness of your wisdom to eradicate any distrust of myself that I may harbor in my mind.

Sometimes I can become so confused that I feel like the inadequate leader, the insufficient leader, the stagnated leader or simply the non-reflective leader. Help me see the true reality of my work and act accordingly in wisdom.

Through your grace, let me surmount any thoughts of being "not good enough."

Unravel my persistent thoughts of personal inferiority, dear Lord, and grant me reprieve from the inaccurate ways I can denigrate and hurt myself.

With your holy light, clear away my cloudy and folly-filled thinking and replace these tendencies with your grace of wisdom.

Help me more fully accept your wisdom and let its truth wash over me and cleanse my soul.

Allow me to join my thoughts with your thoughts, and in this marvelous and loving synthesis, discover your power in me.

Amen

Evening Prayer

Perfectionism

The Compulsion of Wisdom

Save me from my perverted "need" for ever-greater accomplishment.

Lord, let me ask that you reinforce the strength of wisdom that you've already given to me.

I firmly think that with your grace I can overcome any compulsion of chronic dissatisfaction I have with my accomplishments, as well as those unrealistic demands I sometimes place on myself and others.

Lift my thoughts beyond any adolescent need to always be right.

Save me from any twisted "need" for ever-more accomplishment, and internal demands for ever-increasing productivity.

I know that leadership emerges quite naturally when your power and wisdom come together in a new synthesis. Help me reflect on the meaning of this timeless leadership principle and apply it daily in my Servant Leadership role as it unfolds in your holy light Lord.

Grant me the wisdom, Lord, so I can loosen any distorted tendencies of continuously raising my standards and internal demands ever higher to the point of becoming unreasonable and even damaging.

Your wisdom is the only power that frees me from the sadness and anxiety that still seems to cling to me in the many forms that perfectionism can take.

Amen

Morning Prayer

Steadfastness

I find my firmness and determination only in you.

Lord, you are my anchor. I open myself to the world today and know that you are with me forever. What better thought can there be than this?

You fix me in place with you, but I am not stuck, rather this kind of "fixing" paradoxically allows me a new freedom to think with the surety of love and the confidence of your Spirit, the wellspring of all grace.

I move only in you, dear Lord, and while I move closer to you, I also know that this movement brings me to the center of firmness, the site of all power and might.

Lord, I pray that you shower me with the grace necessary to forge ahead with the hard questions that require your leadership, and to do what most needs to be done today.

True leadership only comes from, and is only found in you, dear Lord. I find my firmness and determination only in you as well.

You are unfaltering, and by extension, because of your strength of steadfastness, I can find a secure path to Servant Leadership in you.

Help me come to embrace my utter dependency on you and the steadfast constancy that flows only from you, when I am in sync with your steadfastness.

Your light of purposefulness brightens my soul and brings me to the gates of heaven. In you I am sure.

Amen

Afternoon Prayer

Unreliable

The Shadow of Steadfastness

*I need your light of grace, the grace of steadfastness
to show me the way.*

I am ashamed to admit any lack of self-discipline. How can I escape my shadow of unreliability?

I need your help, dear Lord, especially in my Servant Leadership role to address those times when I can make excuses for what I have failed to do, those times when I hide behind my defensiveness, and even laziness.

I'm overly sensitive to any unreliability that I sense in others; while at the same time I'm blind to it in myself.

My shadow isn't always apparent to me; I can hide it with all my strength because it stands in stark contrast to how I want to see myself.

I so want to be dependable, but I need your light of grace, the grace of steadfastness, to lead my leadership.

I need your strength, Lord, to evaluate what's happening right in front of me; otherwise I can't see the emerging patterns and I consequently ignore the impact they may have for better or for worse.

Help me accept the limits of my capabilities, and save me from all the ways I unknowingly show my unreliability.

Help me shape my thoughts away from irresponsibility—especially any irresponsibility that I previously repressed into unawareness toward you, dear Lord.

Amen

Evening Prayer

Fixated

The Compulsion of Steadfastness

*Let not my hurt become a further fixation
confounding my search for you.*

Dear Lord, help me extract my thoughts from the quicksand of becoming fixated.

I can sometimes become so pre-occupied with meaningless thoughts that I fail to see what is real.

Too easily I avoid even the most obvious and necessary modifications; I need your light of grace to open my darkened mind.

Help me see the value in and the path to a new shared power as the platform for more effective Servant Leadership.

Help me align my thoughts with your thoughts, dear Lord, so that I can grow toward you. Help me develop according to your plan, not my plan.

Help me become clear headed and as free from worldly constraint as possible so I can become more like you, Lord.

Unlock my stubborn thoughts and help me replace them with an eagerness of heart and a vitality of mind.

Help me find steadfastness so I can rid my mind of compulsive thoughts that stagnate me and frustrate my leadership potential.

Let me stand shoulder-to-shoulder with your children in my care and find my path to constructive conversion and growth.

Amen

Morning Prayer

Wholeness

Lord, let wholeness be the point of light today that guides me to your love.

Good morning, Lord, I come to you today to do your will.

My job today is nothing short of bringing your love to my little corner of the world.

I desire nothing more than to live in your love; today that means living in your holy grace of wholeness.

Lord, let wholeness be the point of light that guides me to you today.

Leadership demands wholeness because it involves every facet of my personality. Wholeness gives me the incredible advantage to see the whole system at work as a unit, and not just its many moving parts.

Your wholeness, which you send to me in a channel of grace, is the power that sustains my Servant Leadership goals.

I know that your presence in my mind is divine: intact, complete, and unbroken, yet I live in a world that lacks these things.

Today, with your assistance, I again regroup my thoughts and concentrate only on my one authentic goal: your universal love.

I seek mental coherence, bringing all my disparate thoughts together into an integrated whole, into you. I know that the only perfect wholeness is in you, Lord.

Today I seek your holy wholeness, that sacred state of personality integration.

Amen

Afternoon Prayer

Fragmented

The Shadow of Wholeness

I long to become whole; my thoughts full and undivided.

I am broken; part of my woundedness is my vulnerability to fragmentation of thought.

This shadow of fragmentation causes insecurity that breaks through the otherwise still surface of my conscious mind and disrupts my thoughts; this insecurity can grow into stress and/or strain, and even anxiety.

At times I can even feel mentally scattered, like my thoughts are simply disconnected thought-fragments floating around aimlessly.

Lord, help me recognize when I start slipping toward fragmentation of thought. I want to see the integration better…not the fragmentation, the unity not the division, the whole not the pieces. Servant Leadership requires becoming integrated in thought and whole of being.

I want to melt into your grace-power of wholeness, Lord; I long to become whole—with my thoughts full, developed, and undivided.

I need your grace of wholeness to live in the tension caused by my fear of becoming disconnected from my true self and from you.

I ask for the grace of your wholeness to calm my mind, to give me the strength to find coherence in this disconnected world.

I visualize your light of wholeness illuminating my mind, bringing together all my confused thinking, and giving me peace.

Amen

Evening Prayer

Provincial

The Compulsion of Wholeness

Help me elevate my thinking and be more mindful of living in your presence.

Help me expand my thinking today, Lord; help me transform my dull thoughts into ones that sparkle with your wholeness.

By your grace, save me from thinking thoughts that are too narrow, too shallow, too constricted.

Help me broaden my thinking. Too often my thinking focuses only on the insignificant and meaningless details of daily living.

My thoughts are so often stuck on the tangible plane where confusion reigns; help me transform my thinking to focus on you, Lord.

Without thoughts of you, my mind remains in turmoil, a turmoil that blocks your healing grace of wholeness from finding its intended mark.

Help me elevate my thinking and be ever more mindful of placing myself in the light of your presence more consistently.

Provincialism confines my thinking to small-mindedness. Lord, let me think with your thoughts so I can enlarge all six functions of my personality, and in this sublime openness I can change my heart and soul and move closer to you.

When I think so small, I miss your magnificence and I overlook your grandeur, this blocks me from living in your love, and from being "in love."

I want to find your awe, wonder, and delight that I know is there but which so often escapes me.

Amen

Morning Prayer

Charity

Let me discover your charity today, dear Lord, to give and expect nothing in return.

I awaken thinking of you, Lord, and how you shower me with abundance.

Charity reminds me this morning that this abundance is not just all the giftedness that I think of as "good," but all the rest as well, including all those things, relationships, events, happenings, and thoughts that I formerly considered quite the opposite of good.

All of this is part of your abundance as well.

Help me today, dear Lord, by your unconditional benevolent goodwill of charity to accept every part of your abundance. This includes all the parts that I like, as well as those that I didn't choose but which I know can in some mysterious way encourage my journey to you. Everything is part of your abundance, Lord.

Help me learn the fundamental leadership principle that my goal as a leader is to create an environment that helps all those I serve to shine and find the treasures deep within them. Leadership is not about me!

Let me discover your charity today, dear Lord: to give and expect nothing in return; to help others selflessly; and to recognize other's needs and give generously to them.

Send me your strength of charity today so that I can learn how to love better by shedding any encumbrances that have prevented me from living fully in you.

Amen

Afternoon Prayer

Judgmental

The Shadow of Charity

I need your goodwill, Lord, to save me from chronic criticism.

When I forget my spiritual strength of charity, I drift toward a fearsome coastline that eventually leaves me shipwrecked on the rocks of cynical and negative thinking.

In this cold and barren land I can become opinionated, malevolent, and ill-tempered of thought toward others, toward myself, and even toward you, Lord.

I need your goodwill, Lord, to save me from this chronic criticism, acrimony, and incessant judgment.

Activate my spiritual strength of charity so I can let go of any desire in me to be "the boss," and instead help me empower others with a new capacity of self-giving.

My inner critic works overtime searching the horizon for any bits of data that it can convert into negatives; it bites at the heels of my mind with a vengeance.

Such thinking robs me of the generosity of charity and keeps me cognitively confined to a rancorous resentfulness that sucks your power and might right out of me.

Help me, Lord, to re-establish connection with charity so I can capture your grace, so I can once again find real life in you.

Amen

Evening Prayer

Servitude

The Compulsion of Charity

Let me submit my thoughts only to you, Lord.

Lord, I thank you for the power of charity that helps me give of myself in a selfless manner.

Charity beckons me to submit myself to do your work here on this plane by giving freely to others.

But Lord, help me not submit my thinking to anything else but you.

By the power of charity, help me retain ownership of my thinking and not forfeit it in blind submission to any person or force that is not you and thereby cause me to give up my very self.

I can't compulsively be a leader all the time. I am not playing a robotic role of leader. While I must lead at times, I am much more than this. I am free and clear in my thinking.

Help me hold fast onto my freedom of thought and not lose my liberty of using my mind in your service.

I am your servant only, Lord; by charity, save me from any slavish devotion to another's wishes that may hinder my journey with you.

Save my mind from becoming twisted or confused by some distorted conformity to this world.

Give me the strength of charity so that worldly forces don't capture my thinking and make my mind their prisoner.

Let me submit my thoughts only to you, Lord.

Amen

Section Four

The Feeling Function

The Feeling Function

Feelings are the automatic consequence of your thoughts; every thought, or thought bundle, immediately generates a feeling or bundle of feelings. Interestingly, you have the least volitional influence over your personality feeling function than you do of any of the other five functions. However, you do have immense influence over to what degree and how long a feeling takes up residence in you.

So much of your overall emotional health is determined by your feelings, because your feelings determine your mood more than any other personality force. When you feel 'good,' you're generally in a positive mood, and of course the opposite is true as well. You've had down days, sad times, a sour disposition, and a dour temperament at times. Depression, chronic or cyclical feelings of sadness, anger, irritability or just plain melancholia, seems part of the fabric of life (page 148, <u>Discover Your Spiritual Strengths: Find Health, Healing & Happiness</u>).

Morning Prayer

Joyfulness

I am filled with awe and wonder; I'm bursting with your joy.

Oh happy day, you are here with me still, standing straight and tall at my center.

Let me find your holy delight today, Lord. I wish to live fully in your happiness of heart.

I am jubilant all day—feeling your love as my only reality and my only work today.

Your grace of joy sustains me today and sends my heart into a free-spirited elation.

I am so filled with awe and wonder that I can hardly contain myself; I'm bursting with your joy.

Even when this world weighs heavily upon me, even when it pushes and prods me, attacks me, and disappoints me; even in these dark times, my heart remains joyful knowing that you alone heal me.

I can actually feel joy in my leadership when I incorporate my energy and spiritual strengths into the system of my organization.

Joyfulness is your holy light in me that leads me away from emotional turmoil and toward your calm healing waters.

Joy conquers sorrow by lifting my spirits up beyond the cares of this world and resting them gently on you.

Amen

Afternoon Prayer

Dejection

The Shadow of Joyfulness

I feel dejected at times, but I cannot be dejected because I can only be with you.

Save me from sadness of heart and spirit, Lord. Instead of sadness, I accept your fullness of heart by your power of joy.

When I find myself emotionally flat, perk me up with your effervescent joy. I submerse myself in your pool of joy that washes any dreary feelings away; I emerge fully cleansed of heart and soul.

Your joy dislodges my scales of gloom and dismay; they slide from my shoulders—giving me spirited relief and healing.

Your light pushes out all dark brooding, sulking, and dismal feelings and gradually brings me back to my center, back to joy.

Even in the midst of these dark days I can still feel joy knowing that you never leave me, you never abandon me. Lord, you carry me on your shoulders over my toughest times.

I feel dejected at times, but I cannot be dejected because I can only be with you. Lord, today help me lead with a compassionate heart, and not a dejected one.

Even when I walk the edges of depression, you are there with me holding a lantern that gives me direction and warms my heart.

Amen

Evening Prayer

Hyperphoria

The Compulsion of Joyfulness

Help me confront the low times, which may have much to teach me.

At times I fear losing control of my feelings, like a roller coaster about to fly off the tracks.

With the power of true joy, help me turn away from the compulsion to slide into excessive exuberance that sometimes seems to take over my heart.

Help me realize that I need the calm of being centered; help me regain my heart's true desire and not always yearn for a rush of energy.

True interior joy calms my mood so I can once again return to you at my center.

Lord, help me avoid my proclivity to sometimes become overheated in my emotional responses, so I can lead from my center and not my compulsions.

Help me confront the low times, which may have much to teach me, and not try to flee from them into any excessiveness.

Slow me down, Lord, and give me your power to be more intentional with my feelings and not throw caution to the wind.

Your light of joy can heal my feelings that sometimes threaten to sweep me away into an illusionary place where I lose my bearings because you're not there, Lord.

Amen

Morning Prayer

Trust

Today I wish to fall into you because you are enough for all my needs today, Lord.

I open my eyes this morning confident of your care all day long.

The strength of my feelings for you, Lord, moves me beyond mere belief in your love for me all the way to an assured knowing of your love for me.

Today, I trust.

Thank you for illuminating my emotions out of the darkness of seeking security in this world—a place where there is no certainty—to the only true security which exists in you.

Today I wish to fall into you because you are the abundant provider. You are both necessary and sufficient for all my needs today, Lord.

I cannot trust in me or in anything else; I can only trust in you. There are no guarantees except you, Lord.

Your universal love is my sure light that penetrates through my darkness and heals me. Lord, I need your lead to show me the leverage points for positive change.

I have no doubt that your promise of abundance is being fulfilled even now, as always.

In absolute assurance, I give my life over to you forever.

Amen

Afternoon Prayer

Insecurity

The Shadow of Trust

Let me find your light of assurance, the light that envelops me and heals my illness.

Dear Lord, by your holy trust save me from the times when I'm emotionally shaky, times when I feel unfastened and free-floating with nothing to hold onto.

Lord, help me find your stability when I feel so unstable, as though I stand on quaking ground.

Lord, help me reach for your hand when I feel all confidence draining from me. I search for some surety, a solid place where I can escape feeling so vulnerable and unprotected.

Give me the energy and trust to be continuously orient myself for leadership improvement; because leadership begins on the inside of me, I cannot lose sight of trust and falter into insecurity.

Save me, Lord, from the pangs and fears of anxiety that squeeze whatever meager resolve I possess right out of me.

I can feel so inept when I lose heart; my confidence slips from me, and my determination departs. You are my security, Lord.

At times like these I feel like running away from life, hiding from the terrible critique that I fear lurks around every corner.

Help me, Lord, always remember that you are my sure refuge and my solid strength.

Amen

Evening Prayer

Reductionism

The Compulsion of Trust

Lord, help me trust your voice within me.

Lord, help me stay steady in your trust.

Let me not reduce your trust into adolescent formulas and simplistic solutions for living my life.

Let me keep rules and regulations in proper perspective and not pervert them into inflated demands for perfection, only shallow substitutes for trust in you.

Redirect my vulnerability toward seeking black-and-white answers to questions; you cannot be reduced to a duality. You, Lord, are the fullness of space and time, the Alpha and the Omega.

Help me not slide into always wanting outside authority to lead my heart; instead, help me trust your voice within me.

Help me capture the power and might of trust that opens up my feelings so I can embrace constructive change and not always look to past solutions as the superior answer to questions of my heart.

Help me look forward to the newness of you and not only to the past where tired and worn-out answers cannot satisfy me today.

Lord, energize my leadership by focusing primarily on working networks and away from hierarchies.

Amen

Morning Prayer

Love-Finder

I feel your love all around me.

Love is everywhere this morning, and my job today is to find it.

I look only for the true reality of you, Lord.

I seek the majesty of your awe, the mystery of your wonder, and the magnificence of your delight today.

The power and beauty of your love gives me everything—both inside and out—a sparkling patina that reflects your indwelling presence.

I feel your love all around me, under me, above me, beside me, in front of me, and behind me.

I am surrounded by love and innervated by love. Help me remember that constructive leadership is essentially loving; it's about more vital life and heightened motivation, not a stumbling block made of fear and hesitation.

Help me detect your love in everyone I meet today; let me see you in their eyes, hear your voice in them, and discern the glow of their saintly light.

I am drawn to your light of love as it gently touches every part of me.

I plunge into your love today, and I feel refreshed.

Amen

Afternoon Prayer

Fault-Seeker

The Shadow of Love-Finder

Help me beyond my penchant toward being critical and negativistic.

Lord, help me look away from all the blemishes that I find in myself and others.

Let your strength beckon me away from focusing on defects and imperfections and instead focus on your love reflected on this beautiful, yet imperfect earthly plane.

Help me look past the folly and foibles of this world to the freedom and fascination of your love where I can find my true self.

Help me build my leadership style on the best from my heart and mind, and away from taking on a controlling edge.

With your strength, help me over my penchant toward being sometimes critical and negativistic. Forgive me, Lord, when I'm sarcastic and sneering.

Instead, allow me to feel the warmth of your light of health, healing, and holiness.

Let me give up my distorted dualistic expectations and realize that I don't need to be superlative to escape my critique of being a failure.

Your strength of love-finding lights my way over the dark bridge of pettiness and pessimism to your bright land of loving where I can release the weight of anger.

Amen

Evening Prayer

Pollyannaism

The Compulsion of Love-Finder

I cannot turn my back on the world that needs my strength.

While love is everywhere, I am still in this world and need to recognize its basic brokenness. I can neither overlook the pain of strife nor the bleakness of sin that is folded into the fabric of the human condition.

Help me not disregard the fact that shadows and compulsions can spin me out of control and cause unmeasured damage in my work place and every arena of life.

I cannot turn my back on the world that needs my strength. I cannot exclude, reject, or overlook the callousness and even horror of human action where it rejects your love, Lord.

Help me get past my compulsion to become so overly optimistic that I miss the most important changes that need to be addressed. Help me lead by paying better attention to what's most important now.

Help me respond to your call by first taking off my rose-colored glasses that can at times blind me to the needs of those I lead.

I see the love that is everywhere, but I also feel the degradation of the human soul caused by brutality, greed, and pride.

I accept the challenge of your love to use my strengths not just for my own betterment but also for the good of all those I lead.

Amen

Morning Prayer

Empathy

Let me be exquisitely sensitive to the needs of others and to my own needs as well.

Dear Lord, grant me the strength of empathy today.

Allow me access to your beautiful sensitivity of heart so that I might be fully present to your children in their deepest need.

Let me bear the heartache of others even when the pain threatens to disrupt me.

Let me be exquisitely sensitive to the needs of others and not forget my own needs as well.

Let me be moved by distress, touched by tragedy, and affected by the woundedness in this world.

Yet, also dear Lord, let me celebrate in your good news, delight in the joys of others, and stand in awe of your wonder that I might otherwise overlook. This is, after all, a beautiful world still.

Allow me to open my heart and be thoroughly open and accepting to my role as a leader who truly serves "my" people so we can together accomplish our mission and fulfill our purpose.

Let me be devout in honoring all feelings as reminders of the goodness that I know, without question, throbs in the hearts of all your children.

Amen

Afternoon Prayer

Obtuseness

The Shadow of Empathy

Let me always be emotionally intuitive.

Lord, help me surmount all my vulnerabilities toward insensitivity.

Let me emotionally engage with others and not remain impassive; offer a warm not a cold heart; and render a soft not a callous touch.

As the shadows get longer in the late afternoon, let me not forget to offer these life-giving sensitivities to myself as well.

I have hardened my heart to myself too often and have suffered the sting of self-rebuke, instead of the balm of consolation.

Let me not avoid the reality of my emotions or those of others.

Emotions possess your power, dear Lord; help me value them even in the stressed and wounded state I find myself.

Let me open more fully to your strength of empathy in me and find the true power of your emotional intelligence that is resident therein, Lord.

Let me be emotionally intuitive so I can advance my leadership growth as a journey away from self-centered isolation and toward more sensitive concern for those I lead.

Amen

Evening Prayer

Ingratiating

The Compulsion of Empathy

I need to place this compulsion of always needing praise from others on your altar of healing.

Dear Lord, help me overcome my tendency to contort myself to gain another's favor.

Help me become more aware of the times, places, and people when, where, and whom I subject to this unfortunate tendency.

My exaggerated need to be liked can sometimes be so strong that I submerge my true self and show only what I feel others want from me.

I fear that I am sometimes like a chameleon—changing "colors" not to fade into the background, but to stand out or be liked.

I can over-depend on others for feeling good about myself. Help me to find true joy in you and you alone.

My heart breaks when I recognize this vulnerability at work in me, but even this compulsion I need to place on your altar of healing so I can remain in touch with the true self you have created in me.

Lord, I need the grace of your true empathy so I can be less inclined toward giving pep talks and more concerned with nurturing an animated work environment.

I know I do not need to do anything to win your acceptance, Lord; but help me to seek only your love, which will wash over me and cleanse me.

Amen

Morning Prayer

Gratitude

The light of gratitude pulsates in praise as it makes its rounds through me.

I awaken in profound thankfulness for another day, Lord.

I bow my head and bend my knee; without you I can do nothing.

My very personality is animated only by your power and your gifts, Lord.

Today is a day of 'thank you,' a day of tribute to you.

The light of gratitude pulsates in praise as it makes its rounds through me —searching for and eliminating any misguided emotions that could pull me away from you.

Let me always remember how indebted I am to you, Lord; you know all about me and know particularly what I need now in my life.

I stand in reverence this morning basking in your overwhelming abundance.

I so appreciate your light of gratitude as it instructs me in the difference between authority and true leadership.

I praise your name all the days of my life…forever.

Amen

Afternoon Prayer

Blaming

The Shadow of Gratitude

Lord, help me get past my ridiculing heart.

Lord, why is it so easy for me to feel blame and also to place blame on others?

What is this confusing hold that blame has upon me?

Sometimes I can be so pointed in my speech; at other times I have to fight to keep my condemning attitude at bay.

I don't see myself as critical; I'm actually overly sensitive to critique from others, and yet I'm strangely drawn to participate in blame mostly in my own heart, but sometimes even publicly.

I don't understand this paradox, Lord, but I feel the need to invite your healing grace of gratitude into my life. I ask for your light of healing that alone can warm me with forgiveness and peace.

Leadership means turning toward others in appreciation, and forging deeper relationships of value and worth.

I reprove myself for being even slightly invested in blame, both at myself and at others.

Lord, grant me the gratitude to get past my ridiculing heart, help me beyond my biting thoughts and feelings, and return me to my center point in you.

Amen

Evening Prayer

Submissiveness

The Compulsion of Gratitude

*Help me stand as tall as you made me and not sink
into fawning submissiveness.*

Help me be grateful, Lord, for all that you have given me, rather than so
diminishing of these gifts even to the point of denying them.

I put myself 'down' without even realizing it at all.

Help me stand as tall as I can, as tall as you made me, and not sink into
fawning submissiveness.

My emotions automatically put others ahead of me, as though they were
somehow better than I am.

Sometimes I can feel emotionally paralyzed by a sense of inferiority that
I know in my heart isn't true, and yet it paces like a caged tiger in me.

I feel your grace of gratitude as it moves me to practice the art of
leadership beyond the science of leadership.

Lord, I ask your help in moving from the emptiness of submissiveness to
the fullness of your grace of true gratitude.

Help me move beyond a dispiriting feeling that I should somehow
apologize for my vague feelings of unworthiness.

Help me get past my illusionary over-attempts to be as good as I see
others as being, and divert these feelings of chronic unworthiness to my
advancing journey with you.

Amen

Section Five

The Deciding Function

The Deciding Function

It's been said that life is a series of decisions, decisions, and more decisions. Making decisions can be perplexing. Yet making decisions is not an option if you want to live fully and find fulfillment in leadership.

Leadership requires strength, and strength is derived from personal power. All change—especially change required for leadership and spiritual deepening—requires an attitude of surrender to the power of the Most High. Surrender requires a decision. Leadership demands self-control and self-discipline, all ingredients of the deciding function of your personality. Decisions position you so that Servant Leadership healing can become a working reality in your life.

We all have personal power; the question is to what degree we have we tapped into our own personal power by making prudent choices (page 179, <u>Discover Your Spiritual Strengths: Find Health, Healing & Happiness</u>).

Morning Prayer

Harmony

Help me shape my goals so they all point to living in sync with you.

This morning holds every promise.

As I open my eyes I encounter you first, Lord.

The advancing light creates an eager readiness in me to receive you anew.

My awakening consciousness reminds me that my only agenda today is to be in harmony with you alone.

You are my companion all day long; your light guides me in all my leadership decisions. As a true Servant Leader my choice is to live and work with others, and not seek to dominate the work environment.

Help me find solace in your harmony as the central principle of my life.

Give me the internal harmony so peace can grow verdantly in the sacred garden at my core.

Help me shape my goals so they all point to living in sync with you.

You are the cohesiveness of my heart and the glue holding my will together.

Harmony creates the strong bond that keeps me close to you and helps me take on your goals as my own.

Amen

Afternoon Prayer

Chaos

The Shadow of Harmony

I know that true order comes only from you; I wish to surrender to your order.

Sometimes I feel like I'm coming apart.

I feel chaotic when I have no solid goals, when I lack direction, and when my purpose is confused.

Let harmony instruct me that true leaders are refined in crisis...they are made better. How I learn to work with crisis defines my leadership value.

Save me, with your strength of harmony, from my tendencies toward internal disorder, disorganization, and clutter of soul.

My life needs order, Lord; I know that ultimate order comes only from you, and I so sorely wish to surrender to your order.

Sometimes I can feel so fragmented...a free-floating anxiety that my life could fall into pieces; I even fear that sometimes it already has, and I haven't been paying attention.

I need to "get my head together," to find my center in you, Lord.

I need to be grounded in you, to find my stability and security in you, Lord, the wellspring of harmony.

Help me find integrity of body, clarity of mind, and solidity of spirit, so that with the power of your grace I can surrender this terrible confusion, which I feel inside me over to you—the only one strong enough and big enough to take it in.

Amen

Evening Prayer

Equivocation

The Compulsion of Harmony

My overheated conscientiousness prevents me from finding harmony in you.

Lord, save me from the paralysis of personal doubt, the pain of somehow feeling that I will fail. I know I can't fail when my decisions reflect your will for me.

Relieve my endless hesitation of will—trying to decide the absolute "right" course of action. I know you are the only course I want to follow.

My overheated conscientiousness can keep me in turmoil and prevent me from finding harmony in you.

Help me get beyond the terrible tendency to always "keep my options open" and hence never find a solid place to make a genuine and complete commitment to you.

I know that this confusion of indecision blocks me from being the leader that I want to be. Lord, help me mobilize your resources in me so I can stop equivocating and lead others to deal with the most pressing problems that face us.

I fear making the wrong decision and so I find myself trying to avoid making any decisions at all.

Sometimes I try to please everyone, seeking harmony for all. Of course this kind of harmony is impossible…yet I strive for it anyway.

Lord, pull me away from trying to do too much in a frantic effort to satisfy everyone.

Amen

Morning Prayer

Patience

I calmly continue in you, Lord, whatever the adversity or hardship.

Good morning, Lord. My only goal today is to tap into the mysterious calm of your creation, to listen to the middle "C" note of your immense universe in perfect pitch.

Today I wait only in your time not my time. Help me be patient, Lord, so I can discover how your Spirit in me can find expression in my leadership.

I long to live at my serene center point. There is the only place where I can find true composure.

Lord, help me become ever more mindful of the "process" of living rather than becoming frustrated with the "product" of living.

I calmly continue in you, Lord, whatever adversity or hardship, whatever difficulties, or whatever distractions may befall me.

I long to enter into, and remain in, that still point of your tranquility today, regardless of the gongs and sirens, flashing lights, and pandering calls that I may encounter.

I calmly keep my sight firmly affixed on your steady and sure light of patience, where I find the direction that illuminates my soul and activates my leadership skills.

Amen

Afternoon Prayer

Impulsivity

The Shadow of Patience

Healing occurs in your time, Lord: I cannot force it no matter what I do.

The world wants decision and action "right now."

Help me, Lord, with your patience, to live in your NOW, your ever-immediate love, and not be pushed from my center by an over-demanding world.

I know I must live in the linear time of the material world, but help me avoid being so captivated by the impulsiveness of the world marketplace that I forget that it's only in your eternal time that I find my real life.

Help me endure my sometimes wild inner tendencies to jump to conclusions too quickly as a means of dealing with my own leadership insecurities and uncertainties.

Healing occurs in your time, Lord; I cannot force it no matter what I do.

Help me step back, Lord, and let go of my time-stressed goals; help me move away from my unrealistic agenda and let your Spirit lead me.

Stepping back, letting go, and moving away from impulsivity are my healing choices today.

With the strength of your patience, I can respond rather than react; I can thoughtfully consider rather than hastily jump in.

I patiently commit to your plan, Lord, and give over my own.

Amen

Evening Prayer

Unresponsiveness

The Compulsion of Patience

Lord, give me the patience to make the decisions I must.

Patience is one of your gifts to me, but sometimes I can pervert your wondrous gift, Lord.

Save me from over doing patience to the point of becoming unresponsive to your will. I can sometimes slip into a sluggishness of mind and action and an indolence of decision.

At these times when I place my life on hold, I don't make decisions; it's like I'm numb to my needs and the needs of others (especially those close to me).

Lord, help me focus on what you're asking of me…I sometimes can become deaf to the decisions I need to make.

Give me the patience to break through my unresponsiveness and make the decisions I must.

Sometimes I can be simply lazy; sometimes I don't want to disrupt my comfortable lifestyle; sometimes I just want to remain in my "own world," while at other times I'm just confused.

Compulsions like these block you, Lord, from guiding my leadership and hinder my growth in your Spirit.

Help me with your patience to surmount any tendencies toward inaction, especially when I need to make leadership decisions.

Amen

Morning Prayer

Strength

Your strength is the potent grace that illuminates my soul and brings blessed healing.

I look around my life this morning and realize that you are my only direction, Lord; you are the sole fountain of strength.

I so need your strength, Lord; I rely on you for the fortitude to keep going, for the power and might that you alone can give.

Help me develop a strong commitment to be a leader who serves people and not quashes or overpowers them.

Your strength is that point of light and grace that illuminates my soul and brings blessed healing. Help me mobilize people—with your gift of strength—to address adaptive change.

I always want to keep you as my primary goal, Lord.

Your strength is my power for constructive change, for transformation of my soul that sorely needs healing.

Your strength animates me; it gives me solace knowing that nothing can truly harm me when I live in your strength, Lord.

Today help me clarify my goals so I can walk a straight path in your strength.

I need your strength to pull me through, to give me direction, to provide me with a plan that will sustain me especially during this difficult time.

Lord, grant me the capacity for sustained exertion…only in your strength.

Amen

Afternoon Prayer

Impotence

The Shadow of Strength

I can sometimes feel so rudderless and incapable, so incompetent and insufficient.

Lord, I am weak; without you I lack the stamina to carry on.

Grant me your strength to overcome the horrid powerlessness that overtakes me at times, robbing me of my resolve and morale, and stripping me of trust in you.

I seem so often overcome by fear and doubt; I fear I lack the necessary determination and volition to surrender to your holy lead.

Help me lead from strength, and to learn to speak from my strengths to the strengths of others, and not falter in an illusionary weakness.

I lack the strategies for healing; I see no options for escaping from this vortex of fear that threatens to pull me under.

I can sometimes feel so rudderless and incapable, so incompetent and insufficient.

I know this is all groundless, yet I fall prey to the viciousness of the shadow of impotence, and feel that I have nowhere to turn.

Help me always turn to you, Lord. Send your light of strength to illuminate my capacity to grow beyond exhaustion, beyond demoralization, and beyond paralysis of spirit.

Amen

Evening Prayer

Brutishness

The Compulsion of Strength

Help me make the choices that you would make, Lord.

Sometimes I can make such stupid choices.

When I'm pressed by fear or frustration and/or pushed by pain or loss, I can, without even being aware of it, become heavy-handed with others and with myself.

I can become short, indelicate, and even terse in my responses.

Help me make the choices that you would make, Lord. Sometimes my choices lack true consideration for all concerned; they can be self-serving, blunt, and even hurtful.

My intentions are not malicious, rather I fear appearing weak; I try to over-compensate by merely appearing strong, but I can overdo it.

Save me from any tendencies toward brutishness, Lord, in whatever forms it may take.

Help me align my will with your will; I know that you want the best for me.

I pray that you shore me up with your grace of strength so that I can accept your healing at those times when brutishness may push me to attempt to control others rather than lead others, and to criticize others rather than learn to depend upon them.

Amen

Morning Prayer

Transcendence

*Today I move beyond the realm of simply "doing"
and enter the realm of "being."*

As I awaken from my slumber, I ask you, dear Lord, to show me the mystical ways of transcendence; that I am, at one and the same time, both <u>in</u> this world but I am not <u>of</u> this world.

Healing requires that I join with you in making decisions from the highest reality, from your reality, dear Lord, the most real reality there is.

Today I move beyond the realm of simply "doing" and enter the realm of "being."

Good leadership principles always flow from spiritual strengths; they call me to transcend myself and to move away from the desires of my worldly ego; they transcend my shadows and compulsions and accent my own spiritual strengths.

I want to join my will with your will, dear Lord; this requires that I live fully in both the material world and the spiritual realm at the same time.

As I do, I find that I become fundamentally changed. I am transformed. You bring me beyond the material and invite me to begin walking the outer lawns of your numinous plane.

I am both here on this earth and also with you at the same time.

Your transcendence causes a core shift in me, a shift toward you.

Amen

Afternoon Prayer

Worldliness

The Shadow of Transcendence

*Help me make decisions not as the world makes them,
but as you make them.*

Dear Lord, help me sever the pull that this world has on me; help me move away from living only in this world, being a citizen of this world only, and seeing my roles and personal definition only as the world sees me.

I know that I am so much more than what the world says that I am, I am your child first and foremost.

Let me decide to break free of the way the world sees me and instead choose the option of seeing myself as you view me.

Help me make the commitment to invite your healing power into my leadership role by making decisions not as the world would make them, but as you would make them.

Help me, Lord, have but one true leadership priority: growing toward the singular authority of you.

When I come to a fork in the road and must decide which one to take, help me use your strength of transcendence in me to choose the path that you would have me take.

I can be so mindlessly dazzled and thoughtlessly confused by the world and what it has to offer, to such a degree that I'm blinded to the treasures that you offer.

Help me keep my halo straight today, dear Lord.

Amen

Evening Prayer

Unreality

The Compulsion of Transcendence

Help me find myself again in the truest reality...your reality.

Stir up my strength of transcendence, dear Lord, and save me from constructing fantasies and illusions.

With little or no awareness of the process I use, nor the fantasies I create, I find myself wanting things, relationships, events, and miracles that lack your rational sense and order.

While genuine leadership does call me to venture out beyond the safe and familiar, my objective is to always remain in what's real, and not head into fantasy.

Let me see the true reality of love as my standard for making decisions.

Let me move beyond my illusionary expectations that create unreality and grab onto the solid and sure handhold that you offer me, dear Lord.

Free me from making unrealistic commitments that I cannot keep.

Lead me away from fantasies, Lord. Help me stay centered in your transcendence and there discover your power to heal any brokenness or lack of leadership.

Keep me away from the land of unreality where I'm blinded to the true discernment of spirit that comes only from you.

Help me find myself again in the truest reality...your reality.

Amen

Morning Prayer

Self-Discipline

I pray that I may have the power to focus only on your point of light of self-discipline.

This morning I decide to truly surrender my ego, my worldly self, over to you. In so doing, I open myself up to your divine direction.

I seek to be obedient only to you, Lord.

My ego-self wants me to choose the siren's song and pandering voice of the world. I know this brings me only separation from you and causes my hurts to flourish.

Help me be in allegiance with you first, Lord. Help me seek you first and place your will for me as the true north of my being.

I pray that I may have the power to accept your point of light of self-discipline and embrace your ongoing healing.

Help me, Lord, to follow your leadership goal: to be disciplined enough to make a difference in the world.

Help me to seek your grace of self-discipline alone, rather than circling the drain of self-indulgence.

You create the splendor in me, Lord, and through your power of self-discipline in me, you allow me to achieve new heights of wholeness otherwise unattainable.

Amen

Afternoon Prayer

Self-Indulgence

The Shadow of Self-Discipline

Bring order to my mind, calmness to my heart, and determination to my will.

Lord, I can falter.

I can too easily be swept up in the whirlwind of the bling and tinsel of the world.

Help me say "no" to those nagging forces of inertia that bite at my resolve; help me follow you more nearly.

Help me open to your divine discipline that can heal the world.

I need to always grow toward becoming a leader who serves rather than one who expects to be served.

Help me wipe laziness, idleness, and inactivity from me. Lord, guide me away from my dolt-like lack of self-control.

Bring order to my mind, resolve to my heart, and determination to my will.

Help me see when enough is enough, and that I needn't yearn for more.

Help me be satisfied in you and turn away from the enticing excesses that my ego desires.

I ask for your mighty grace of self-discipline so I can get a firmer grip on my inner urges that can move off my center.

In you I trust, Lord.

Amen

Evening Prayer

Self-Repression

The Compulsion of Self-Discipline

Help me recognize that this senseless self-control is not your will for me.

Lord, while I can sometimes be self-indulgent, at other times I can pervert your grace of self-discipline and cross over into self-repression.

This, of course, is not my intention, not my objective, but nonetheless by some distortion of desire, I give myself too many "shoulds."

Self-repression pushes me toward becoming a top-down leader rather than one who stands squarely with others.

I can, at times, demand too much from me—I push for unattainable achievement; I impose stricture on myself that defies reason and constricts me.

Lord, free me from this self-imposed drive where I demand more and more of me with relentless disregard for balance.

Help me recognize that this excessive self-control is not your will for me, but only my contorted desire to hold down the terrible fear of failure that sometimes infects my soul.

I need your light of self-discipline to release me from my own self-suppression of will, a repression that blocks your transformative work in me.

I want to find the freedom of your will for me.

May thy will and not my will be done, Lord.

Amen

Section Six

The Acting Function

The Acting Function

All of creation, all that we can see, and the utter vastness of what we can't see, is the result of the action of a powerful hand. The elegantly swirling galaxies, the incomprehensible distance of space, the vibrancy and tenderness of the star nurseries, the terrible power of black holes, and the dazzle of the seas of stars, all bespeak a wonder of divine action so gigantic that far surpasses the tiny limits of the human mind. All of this action is the result of an energetic hand acting at and from the source of all power, a benevolent hand of purpose.

While some action is outward, most is inward. The world cannot see the interior changes in believing, or perceiving, or thinking, or feeling, or deciding; no, the world can only see the exterior change in our behavior...our acting function. Yet, as the carpenter from Nazareth reminds us, "My kingdom is not of this world." My reading of this passage brings me to the fact that the Spirit of God acts most decisively in the bosom of my interior (page 207, Discover Your Spiritual Strengths: Find Health, Healing & Happiness).

Morning Prayer

Truth

Your truth is a lighthouse beacon keeping my direction straight and my actions sure.

I awaken this morning knowing that your truth is in me; that you offer me the grace that sets me free from my own distorted desires, which only feed my hurts.

Your truth elevates my behaviors in accordance with your guiding hand and sustains my actions in line with your divine honesty.

I am like a ship at sea that would be lost except for your truth that shines like a lighthouse beacon keeping my direction straight and my actions sure.

Accompany me as I search for my truth, which, of course, is your truth. I need to find my own truth to be the best leader I can. I need to take the pilgrimage into my depths so I can discover and embrace my true values, motives, and goals.

Your grace gathers up all the little disparate pieces of me and forms them together—giving me integrity of mind and surety of action.

Truth sets me free from the clutter of distraction that encumbers my freedom of action in you.

I desire to be sure and true in you, Lord.

My heart's desire is to follow you all the days of my life and to be your hands and feet in this world.

Help me focus on the light of truth in me, the freedom-giving grace that transforms and refreshes me.

Amen

Afternoon Prayer

Deceit

The Shadow of Truth

Save me from playing with the truth.

Lord, save me from the slippery slope of fooling myself.

When I misplace your truth, I start down a road to self-deception.

I can slide into untruths without any conscious awareness of it until I crash head-on into the darkness of falsehood.

Save me from playing with the truth, manipulating it, and even from telling little "white" lies that can grow into full-pledged self-deception.

Help me to find the light of your truth that I may have blocked out with deceit. This is the light that saves me from confusion.

Lord, help me direct my efforts toward building shared power among my team, rather than opting for more centralized power.

This is the light that illuminates my true intentions and gives resolve to my actions.

Save me from advancing untruths, from giving false witness, from bluffing myself, and from bending or circumventing the truth to achieve undeserved "reward."

Help me to take the risk of recognizing and telling your truth, Lord.

Amen

Evening Prayer

Skepticism

The Compulsion of Truth

Help me move away from doubting and into your light of truth.

I so desire truth that at times I take on an overly-questioning mindset desperately trying to determine if any deception exists.

Skepticism has become my personal "default-position."

I so fear being lied to, being cheated, being gullible, and being seen as foolish that I find it hard to believe almost anything.

Lord, save me from seeing the motivations of others as manipulative, or even malevolent.

Help me move away from doubting and into your light of truth.

I find it so hard to believe others that I begin questioning myself, and forgive me, Lord, I even question your motivations.

I'm dubious and have developed a critical attitude—all in an effort to avoid being deceived.

I need your healing, Lord.

There is no power in this world that can cleanse this terrible curse from my soul; I need the power that only comes from you, the power of truth so I can mobilize the strengths that I know exist in others who look to me for leadership.

Light me up with your truth, Lord; brighten my world and heal me from myself.

Amen

Morning Prayer

Inspiration

Let my actions today be a testimony to your wonder-working power in my soul.

Dear Lord, as the sun gently pushes away the darkness; infuse me with the light of your inspiration.

Illuminate my actions and help me become ever more aware of your presence in everything that I do, and everyone I meet today.

Let your inspirational light show me your real world and be my healing power.

Grant me the gift of inspiration to guide my hands and feet today, so that I can be about your business all day long and act to inspire all whom you send to me.

Motivate me with your inaudible yet clear voice, and let me be the true inspired "me" as I move through this day.

Touch me with your mighty mechanisms of care, so that my actions reflect your healing power to me and to those around me.

Help me, Lord, to let go of any hurt that befuddles me and blocks your healing so that I can be the "you" that you want me to be, and to act in your name to inspire my group to optimal functioning.

Let my actions today be a testimony to your wonder-working power in my soul.

Amen

Afternoon Prayer

Lifelessness

The Shadow of Inspiration

Help me resist the terrible passivity that tugs at my heart.

Oh Lord, I ask for your love-energy of inspiration this afternoon to overpower my proclivity toward lifelessness.

I need your light to overcome the lack of spirit that so often darkens my soul.

Help me resist the terrible passivity that tugs at my heart and dampens the vigor of your inspiration in me.

Let me accept your continuous grace of inspiration so I can act with resolve and purpose today and discover the meaning that you have hidden for me among the folds of my behavior.

Let me become more aware that I am dependent only on you and nothing or no one else.

Inspire my spirit to act as you would have me act today.

I need your inspiration so that I don't slip into an insipid morbidity, and consequently, put on hold what is genuinely most important for our overall mission.

Inspire me, Lord, out of my sometimes flaccid approach to leadership, and show me how to act with your energy.

Amen

Evening Prayer

Excitability

The Compulsion of Inspiration

Grant me release from my need to live my life in constant motion.

Calm my body with your holy inspiration today, dear Lord, so that I may move beyond my desperate need for continuous stimulation.

Infuse my actions with your restful inspiring presence so I may move away from the ferocity of anxiousness and nervousness.

Your inspiration is a light from you that shines within me and heals my tendency toward excitability.

Inspiration propels me to new realms of peace and tranquility, to places of quiet and relaxation where my dismaying agitation is quenched by your soothing quiet words.

Give me the power to stop my perpetual movement with its frantic repetition, which infects my spirit with a terrible monotony as though I were on a treadmill going nowhere, instead of on a purposeful journey toward you.

Grant me release from my need to live my life in constant motion, a frenetic flutter of action going nowhere except to yet more senseless stimulation, all the while living in a wasteland of activity of going only in circles.

Inspire me, dear Lord, so I can once again enjoy your quiet presence in me. Help me remember that leadership is essentially a life-giving activity, both for me and those given to me to lead.

Amen

Morning Prayer

Kindness

You call me to be kind—to demonstrate gentle, affectionate, and loving behaviors.

Lord, today help me learn your ways of kindness.

Help me stay anchored in your kingdom but not forget your children's needs here on this earth as well.

Help me remain ever focused on the light of your grace; that grand and sublime kindness that soothes and heals me.

Help me keep your healing light shining in me all day long.

Lord, you call me to be kind—to demonstrate gentle, affectionate, and loving behaviors. Help me carry this out with a special understanding that my healing requires that I accept your words and carry out the behaviors that flow from this surrender.

Your kindness calls me to help others, but let me not forget to be kind to myself as well.

Help me accept everything, and everyone, including myself, as gifts from you that deserve my holy attention.

Help me always lead by doing and not simply by telling.

Lord, help me to render care where it is needed, friendship where it's called for, and aide where it's most required.

Let me do all of this with respect and courteous goodwill.

Amen

Afternoon Prayer

Neglect

The Shadow of Kindness

Help me realize that my actions can and do make a difference.

I don't intentionally neglect anyone or anything, but I know that I can distance myself from you by my omissions.

Lord, help me to see the passive quality of neglect; it's what I don't do and when I don't act that bites at my soul.

I pray for your grace of kindness so I can give attention to those things, places, and people who need it.

Help me realize that my actions can and do make a difference, however small, and that your face is always present in everything.

Let me not ignore, isolate, or stonewall my efforts or those of others who wish to help.

Help me see how I may benignly neglect my own needs and requirements. Let me not disrespect or deny what is necessary for my continued growth toward you.

Open up my heart so I can be kind to myself during this time of healing.

Any dark tendency of mine toward neglect needs the healing light of your kindness; help me do what I need to do to welcome your grace completely.

Show me, Lord, how to be most useful in how I lead. Steer me away from any form or sense of neglect in my leadership. I am blessed to lead.

Amen

Evening Prayer

Co-Dependency

The Compulsion of Kindness

*Save me from hovering over another in my vain
efforts to make sure that all goes well.*

Lord, help me realize when and how I'm becoming dependent on another person's dependencies.

Save me from over-stretching my efforts to help or support someone else I care for personally or serve professionally.

I can over-function at times and inadvertently and unnecessarily relieve others of responsibility for helping themselves.

Save me from hovering over another in my vain efforts to make sure that all goes well.

Help me let natural consequences bring more reasonable results even though there may be some pain in the short-run.

Help me not smother another but realize that kindness includes letting the other person take responsibility for his/her actions.

I cannot carry someone else's cross; I can only carry my own.

Lord, heal me with your light of true kindness; save me from my proclivities of losing sight of the effects of my actions.

Help me adopt a personal leadership philosophy that can best align my personal vision for growth with the mission of the organization I serve.

Amen

Morning Prayer

Courage

Let your courage saturate my personality.

Lord, the morning light reminds me of the immense internal fortitude that you have given me; you have planted your courage in me.

You call me to accept your healing of my weakness with resilience and hardiness, to hold out against its attacks…to be as tenacious as a bulldog.

Your grace gives me firmness of mind and the courage to venture forth even in the face of danger.

You make me dauntless, Lord.

My role is to open up my doorways of grace, so I can position my true self in such a way as to receive your power and might maximally.

My many hurts are echoes that one day I'm leaving this earth and journeying closer to you, part of my healing is to remember this unalterable fact.

Help me stand against the slings and barbs of my own vulnerability.

Lord, grant me the leadership moral courage to stand straight and tall every day and especially on those days when I'm tempted to listen to voices other than yours.

Let your courage saturate my personality so I may not fall into the temptation of my shadows and compulsions.

Amen

Afternoon Prayer

Timidity

The Shadow of Courage

Let your courage be the point of light that gives me strength to continue.

Lord, I can become scared, faint of heart, and even lose the determination of courage that I know is your gift to me.

Give me the self-confidence to stop avoiding that which I must face; help me not 'run for cover' in the sometimes odd ways that I can.

Let me not shrink from carrying the cross that I need to carry now.

Let your courage be the point of light that gives me strength to continue with inspiration.

Save me from letting fear send me into retreat—evading the hard truth of my woundedness and thereby prolonging the pain that it causes.

I pray for your courage to lift me from my tendency to shy away from what I know I must do, or dodge your sometimes-difficult offers to lead with courage.

Your courage can help me pull my head out of the sand and face fore square all that I need to face.

You are my strength, Lord. You are the light that eases my pain and brings healing.

Help my leadership be a force for positive, transformative change—in my heart and in my behavior with all whom I have served in the past.

Amen

Evening Prayer

Arrogance

The Compulsion of Courage

Give me the courage so I can drink the cup of my woundedness.

I can sometimes show a false courage by unknowingly creeping over into arrogance.

I can cop a condescending attitude and a superior tone.

Help me become more aware of the many ways that I do this and thus avoid the work of your true courage in me.

I can hide behind the bravado of arrogance to cover-up my inadequacies surrounding timidity.

I can puff myself up in an attempt to appear better than I am.

Help me from violations of caution, deliberation, and true consideration, where I am imprudent, careless, and sometimes stumble headlong into unnecessary or ill-conceived actions that I am later forced to defend or clean up after.

Save me from the terrible *hubris* that can contort my soul.

Help me be more like you, Lord, showing the hard courage you did.

Give me that courage so I can drink the cup of leadership. Help me find my real courage and not slip into leadership pathology; an arrogant autocratic style where I'm deaf to the needs of my team members and those I serve.

Amen

Morning Prayer

P e r s e v e r a n c e

Right now, in my hour of need, your perseverance sustains me.

Lord, I open my eyes this morning knowing that I have but one purpose: growing closer to you.

You hold me up with your perseverance, the grace to carry on, and your powerful tenacity in me that leads me to persistently plod on in my quest for you.

I thank you, Lord, for your gift to run the extra mile, to carry on when hope is slim, to stay the course even when I see only darkly through the lens of life.

Right now, in my hour of need, I know your perseverance is there to sustain me.

Your perseverance surprises me because I know that this is not my power, but your power in me that enables me to find healing while carrying this heavy cross.

I know that leadership is a dynamic process of ongoing growth and development, dedication to daily renewal. Perseverance heals my soul.

Perseverance animates my actions and activates my true spiritual grit to keep going and to keep fully on the task of healing with stamina and backbone.

I am filled with awe at the power you have invested in me.

Amen

Afternoon Prayer

Giving Up

The Shadow of Perseverance

Lord, help me stay engaged and not desist.

Oh, how I sometimes want to surrender, not to you, Lord, but to my failings.

I want to withdraw from "action," throw in the towel, and simply walk away.

But then I remember your gift of perseverance. I can then get up, gain my footing, and begin my journey back to you again.

Help me stay engaged and not desist, help me stay in the "game" and not prematurely terminate my efforts before my time.

I can overcome my exhaustion with your perseverance; I can persist and not submit to my vulnerabilities of giving up too soon.

Lord, help me know the difference between the growth of surrendering (falling in) to you, and the stagnation of surrendering to my pain.

Your light of perseverance illuminates my actions so that they point only to you.

Let me not take the counsel of the world and retreat without just cause.

Grant me the perseverance to come to you for healing my desire to throw up my hands in surrender.

Help me renew myself by ever-reminding me that leadership is essentially developing mechanisms of hope and advances to serve, not shrinking from them.

Amen

Evening Prayer

Imperilousness

The Compulsion of Perseverance

Lord, help me see that I don't need to be a martyr.

Lord, help to recognize the times when I am unnecessarily endangering myself and/or others.

I don't want to be in jeopardy, but I fear that, even without my conscious awareness, I can take actions (or inactions) that place what I love in danger.

Save me from these tendencies of action; help me persevere in your love and remain open to your grace that fortifies me in body, mind, and spirit.

Help me see that I don't have to "go down with the ship." I don't need to be a martyr.

Your grace is the only power than can save me from imperilousness, this illogical perversion of your strength of perseverance.

Imperilousness is not strength; on the contrary, it is a compulsive act to get me beyond my fear of giving up.

I know I'm not a quitter, but I needn't prove it to myself or anyone else, and certainly not to you, Lord, by unnecessarily "playing with fire."

Help me to always remember my personal and true leadership style, a style that I take from your model, Lord, which shows me the courageous action of the Spirit.

Amen

Postlude

You must be persistent in your prayer for it to become maximally effective in your walk in Servant Leadership. Regularly and continuously touching your own soul with the Divine increases your receptivity to God's power.

"We are to pray in everyday life, and we are to make everyday life our prayer." (Rahner, p. 45).

As you read through the collection of prayers in this book, and as you journey through your life in prayer, it is important to remember—

- Prayer does not ensure that we will be insulated from the trials and tribulations of Servant Leadership.

- Prayer does not offer an escape hatch from our worldly duties and responsibilities of Servant Leadership.

- Prayer does offer us the spiritual potentials of strength, perseverance, and spiritual stamina so we may remain steadfast in faith and calm of demeanor regardless of the personal travails of our Servant Leadership walk.

- Prayer is our stimulus to grow in the face of human conflict; prayer is not a means of avoiding the conflict itself.

- Prayer offers a magnificent means for vigorously entering into the fray of Servant Leadership and yet, at the same time, prayer offers us a new calmness and a peaceful detachment from the outcome of the fray.

Go in peace to serve the Lord and find immense healing.

Appendix I: How to Best Use This Book

You can use this prayer book in several ways. You can—

- Use it as a one-month self-directed mini-retreat reciting and meditating on each of the 30 sets of three prayers, one set per day for a month.

- Use it as a prayer reference by opening to any page for prayerful inspiration and/or psychological motivation.

- Incorporate it into a more comprehensive, targeted and effective program called the…

Spiritual Strengths Healing Plan

The following steps can help you discover deeper truths about who you are and the strengths God has implanted in you (not to mention the shadows and compulsions that accompany those strengths).

Step 1: Take the Spiritual Strengths Healing Profile

The Spiritual Strengths Healing Profile, which is available at www.SpiritualStrengthsHealing.com, takes about 25-30 minutes to complete and it generates a 20-page personal analysis of your spiritual strengths that gives you a new depth of self-understanding that quite naturally moves you toward healing. You'll discover your six "premier spiritual strengths" as well as the shadows and compulsions that accompany them. These six strengths are the virtues that God has given to you most clearly at this stage in your life so you can make the most of whatever life is bringing you at this time. These six constitute your personal formula for achieving maximal healing.

Step 2: Read the <u>Discover Your Spiritual Strengths</u> Book

Procure the reference book: <u>Discover Your Spiritual Strengths: Find Health, Healing & Happiness</u>. This is the "flagship" book of the SSHP series of books; you will want this book for reference as you move through the Plan. If you want to go even deeper, then proceed to...

Step 3: The Spiritual Strengths Personal Conversion Program

Procure your own Spiritual Strengths Healing Immersion Program on www.SpiritualStrengthsHealing.com. This is an individualized, seven-week program made especially for you based on your specific and unique six spiritual strengths. The Immersion Program asks you to spend about 15 minutes per day for seven weeks. The Program allows God's healing power to penetrate deeply into you. You become saturated as you soak in the warm, cleansing, and healing waters of your spiritual strengths. Your daily time with your spiritual strengths nourishes your heart, mind, and soul in ways that bring you to a brand new level of healing.

Step 4: Prayer

The prayers in this book can be used anytime, anywhere, and in any way you find them helpful. Perhaps the best way to use these prayers is to use them in conjunction with Step #3 (above) by devoting each day of the week to a different one of your premier healing strengths. You are asked to pray your spiritual strength prayer in the morning, its corresponding shadow prayer in the afternoon, and its compulsion prayer in the evening. This organized approach, used in conjunction with the SSHP and the other reading material that is part of the Program, offers you the consistency and regularity that is essential for inviting healing grace into your life.

Step 5: Follow Through

Work through the seven-week program. I know from my clinical experience with hundreds of persons seeking healing that following the 7-Week Immersion Program does bring results.

Appendix II: The Spiritual Strengths Healing Plan

Research I conducted more than several years ago, when I was the Director of Behavioral Sciences at a large teaching hospital, has instructed me well about the movement and effect of God's healing power in our lives. What I eventually found has not only changed my perception of sickness and healing, but has indeed transformed (healed) my entire life as well.

Through this personally moving period in my life, I felt the hand of God on mine, urging me to write what I had seen in these marvelous spiritually-healing patients—a special 15% or so who seemed to embrace their sicknesses with "spiritual gusto" and grace. I became the scribe...I honestly feel that God moved my hands, not in any automatic writing phenomenon, but clearly I was guided to organize what I had observed into a coherent and practical program. Over the years, I have given innumerable healing workshops and talks, all of which helped me refine this organization of ideas and revelations, until it has taken the form it has today, in what I call The Spiritual Strengths Healing Plan.

As I mentioned earlier, many of my insights regarding the SSHP were gleaned while working at a hospital where patients were sick. However, I soon began making a distinction between the *sickness* these patients encountered and their *illness(es)*. So often we use these terms interchangeably as though they each mean the same thing. They don't!

Sickness is when a part of the body is broken or malfunctioning. Any medical diagnosis or psychiatric malady is a sickness. Diabetes, for example, is a sickness.

Illness, on the other hand, refers to personal, emotional, psychological, and/or spiritual reactions *to* your sickness or conditions that have crept into your life due to other circumstances. In fact, taking on the role of a Servant Leader itself can pose such "illnesses" at times.

Therefore, it is my belief that everyone needs healing in one form or another—be it physical, psychological, emotional, or spiritual. The following is a short list of the conditions that can benefit from digging deeper into the SSHP.

- **Physical Sicknesses**: Cancer, heart disease, MS, Lupus, migraine, addictions, hypochondriasis, pain, weight management/loss, smoking cessation, pneumonia, COPD, hypertension, arthritis, immune disorders, Parkinson's, diabetes, stroke, chronic fatigue etc., etc.

- **Psychological Issues**: Anxiety, depression, personality disorders, OCD, manipulation, stress, bi-polar disorder, etc.

- **Emotional Issues:** Being unrealistic, lacking responsibility, low-self-esteem, career focus issues, poor organization skills, family disharmony, anger management, fears, perfectionism, marriage discontent, lifelessness, infidelity, irritability, chronic lateness, caregiving, etc., etc.

- **Spiritual Dis-eases:** Peace of mind and heart, un-forgiveness, existential angst, inner pain, grudges, scrupulosity, incomplete developmental transitions, guilt, grief and unresolved grief, regrets, blame, disappointments, so-called "unfinished business," resentments, etc., etc.

- **Spiritual Direction & Growth:** Gaining better clarity of God's plan in your life, and breaking through barriers that may be hindering your faith journey.

Appendix III: The Spiritual Strengths

The following graphic depicts how spiritual strengths continuously and simultaneously flow from one function of your personality to the next—each accompanied by a shadow and compulsion (mentioned within the prayers of this book). To learn more about your premier Servant Leadership strengths, you can visit the website www.spiritualstrengthshealing.com to take the Spiritual Strengths Healing Profile and/or pick up a copy of <u>Discover Your Spiritual Strengths</u> by Richard Johnson.

Appendix IV: Books in the Spiritual Strengths Healing Series

- God Give Me Strength! Using the Spiritual Strengths Healing Plan

- Discover Your Spiritual Strengths: Find Health, Healing, and Happiness (flagship book of the SS Healing Plan)

- Body, Mind, Spirit: Tapping the Healing Power Within

- Prayers for Healing… Physical Illnesses, Emotional Broken Places, an/or Spiritual Dis-eases

- The Ten Most Effective Spiritual Self-Care Techniques for Healing and Well-Being

- Smiling Through Whatever Life Brings: Using Positive Psychology for Optimal Healing

- Healing Wisdom: 101 Spiritual Truths for Optimal Well-Being

- Healing and Depression: Finding New Peace in the Midst of Transition, Turmoil, or Illness

- Discover Your Spiritual Center: Constructing a Personal Inner Healing Program

- Renew Your Life Direction: Finding Personal Meaning After Sickness, Distress, or Life Transition

Books for Caregivers

- Caregiving from Your Spiritual Strengths: The Ten Fundamental Principles for Optimal Success

- Because I Care… Inspiration for Caregiving: for Spouses, Health Care Personnel, Family & Friends

Appendix V: Assumptions of the Spiritual Strengths Healing Plan

1.   Healing is best understood to proceed along all three levels of human experience: 1) body, 2) mind, and 3) spirit. Maximal healing is achieved holistically—when each of these three levels of human experience are addressed as a part of a whole.

2.   The "mind" portion of the holistic perspective of healing is seen in the SSHP as the six operational functions of your personality: 1) believing, 2) perceiving, 3) thinking, 4) feeling, 5) deciding, and 6) acting.

3.   The "Spirit" portion of the holistic perspective is seen in the SSHP as the special or premier spiritual strength (virtue) you have received in each of the six functions of your personality. You have been given one premier gift in each of the six functions for a total of six spiritual strengths…your special healing type…your spiritual fingerprint.

4.   Love is the fundamental healing power; all energy flows from this central font of the power of Love. Love comes from God; it cannot be manufactured or synthesized by humans.

5.   Healing is clearly distinguished from the medical concept of curing. Curing means restoring physical brokenness or malfunctioning (sickness) to a state of

functionality. Healing, on the other hand, is seen as closing the gap in mind and/or spirit that was opened by your reactions to your sickness. This gap, usually expressed through personality pain, is what is called illness.

6. The more completely you can open up to the healing power of God within you, the more you will benefit from these gifts of grace.

7. You have been endowed with spiritual strengths that are particular, singular, specific, and unique to you.

8. These personal spiritual strengths serve as your primary means of achieving healing and personal spiritual growth.

9. As you become increasingly aware of your spiritual strengths, you will quite naturally begin the process of folding the power of your spiritual strengths into your everyday life.

10. Each spiritual strength has a corresponding shadow, a condition where the spiritual strength is absent. This shadow presents a vulnerability within you.

11. Likewise, each spiritual strength has a corresponding compulsion, a condition where your ego has distended the strength to a point of distortion. This compulsion becomes a proclivity in you to move away from your spiritual strength and consequently away from your Real Self.

12. When shadows are brought to light, and compulsions are revealed as personality "terrorists," healing work begins the work of using your shadows and/or compulsions in service of your healing and enhanced spiritual growth.

13.   The SSHP is not "faith healing" where you rely on your internal mechanisms as the sole means for physical cure. It never promises cure; its purpose is healing. It can however be seen as a supplement and support for traditional medical practices. The philosophy of the SSHP is that you should seek the best and most appropriate medical and psychological care you can in accord with your own personal wishes.

References

Baron, Tony, Ph.D., The Art of Servant Leadership: Designing Your Organization for the Sake of Others, Wheatmark, Tucson, AZ, 2010.

Blanchard, Ken and Hodges, Phil, <u>The Servant Leader</u>, Countryman (Div. of Thomas Nelson), Nashville, TN, 2003.

Businessballs management information website: Leadership Theories page – see "leadership terminology definitions – models, philosophies, styles" section: http://www.businessballs.com/leadership-theories.htm 2012-02-24. Retrieved 2012-08-03

Gillet, J., Cartwright, E., & Van Vugt, M. (2010). Selfish or Servant Leadership: Testing evolutionary predictions about leadership in coordination games. Personality and Individual Differences.

"Five Steps to Increasing Employee Motivation". Jpmaroney.com.

James A. Autry, <u>The Servant Leader</u>, Three Rivers Press, NY, 2001.

Jim Collins, <u>Good to Great</u>, HarperCollins Books, Inc., New York, 2001.

Sharon Daloz Parks, <u>Leadership Can Be Taught</u>, Harvard Business School Press, Boston, 2005.

Leonard Doohan, <u>Spiritual Leadership: The Quest for Integrity</u>, Paulist Press, Mahway, NJ, 2007.

Robert K. Greenleaf, <u>Trustees as Servants</u>, The Greenleaf Center for Servant Leadership, 1976.

Richard P. Johnson, <u>Discover Your Spiritual Strengths</u>, AGES Press, St. Louis, MO, 2008.

Richard P. Johnson, <u>Prayers for Spiritual Strength</u>, AGES Press, St. Louis, MO, 2013.

Kent M. Keith, <u>The Case for Servant Leadership</u>, The Greenleaf Center for Servant Leadership, 2008.

Karl Rahner, <u>Encounters with Silence</u>, Newman, 1999.

Sipe, James, W. & Frick, Don, M., Seven Pillars of Servant Leadership: Practicing the Wisdom of Leading by Serving, Paulist Press, Mahwah, NJ, 2009.

Stephen Tutas, SM, keynote address given at leadership conference, Menlo Park, CA, Oct. 3, 2013.

Staehle, W.H.: Management, p. 842.

Scouller, J. (2011). The Three Levels of Leadership: How to Develop Your Leadership Presence, Knowhow and Skill. Cirencester: Management Books 2000.

"Ten Ways to Improve Employee Satisfaction". Retrieved 2012-08-09.

"The Understanding and Practice of Servant Leadership." Regent University. August 2005. Retrieved 2012-08-09.

"Throw Out the Script: Improvisation, Innovation, and Servant Leadership".servantleadershipinstitute.com. Retrieved 2013-10-13.

Wikipedia: "Servant Leadership."

Made in the USA
San Bernardino, CA
21 August 2014